SPY

Manual

LOADS FOR YOUNG SPIES TO MAKE AND DO

Andrew Parkinson

CONTENTS

Getting started 1

Spy's toolkit 2

Cool codes 3

PASSPORT

United States of America

SPY
Manual

Manual

INTRODUCTION

The *Spy Manual* has masses of information to teach you how to be the best spy ever. There's loads of cool equipment to make and use. There are codes and methods to confuse the enemy. There are tricks that'll impress your family and friends. And there are lots of fun games and challenges, too.

All the activities are explained clearly, and there are masses of photos to show you exactly what to do. With the help of the *Spy Manual*, you'll soon be enjoying the exciting world of espionage in your own home and neighbourhood!

The *Spy Manual* will teach you how to be a brilliant spy. There could be enemies in your area and baddies in your back yard, but with the help of this book you'll be able to confuse and outwit them. You're going to get a peep into a dangerous world and learn vital secrets to survive.

To be a super spy, you'll be learning here how to:

▷ Hide messages in all sorts of ways

▷ Trick your enemies

▷ Make cunning gadgets to outwit your enemies

▷ Make weapons to protect your family and friends

▷ Be very observant – this means looking at things very carefully

▷ Use codes and clever messages to confuse the enemy

This book is full of great ideas for you to use. But remember, some of them are top secret. There are codes and tricks that would be ruined if they fell into the wrong hands. Do you really know who your friends are? Then you can let them into these secrets. But make sure none of this reaches any enemy HQ! Now, what would you like to do first? Read on ...

Watch out!

Difficult to do?

On each project, you'll see these marks. They show how difficult each project is, from one mark for fairly easy and quick, to five marks for hardest and longest.

Difficulty rating	🔒 🔒 🔒 🔒 🔒

Adult help?

You may find that you need a little help for some of these projects – especially the ones marked with this sign.

ADULT HELP NEEDED

Cutting out?

Turn to the back of the manual to find detailed instructions for cutting out the paper or card you'll need to make some of the projects.

SEE CUTTING DIAGRAM ON PAGE 100

Getting started as a spy

So you want to be a spy? You're going to learn a lot. And one of the first things to learn is being good at keeping secrets! Your first important secret could be your codename. Make sure only your most trusted friends and family know what it is...

Who are you going to be?

One of the first things you need is a codename. Codenames are special names given to things, people and activities. You and your friends need to decide on codenames, to hide who you are and what you're up to. If your enemies hear the codenames, you want to be sure they don't know what they mean!

Single-letter names

All the spies in this book have special code letters. Why those particular letters? Well, only their close family and friends will know who they are. This is because they've used the first or last letters of their middle names, for example, Agent T's middle name is Theo. You could use the first letter of your first name, but that might be a bit obvious to your enemies. So if you have a middle name, make use of it.

Police-alphabet names

You can make initials more interesting, using an alphabet the police use. They say Alpha for A, Bravo for B, and so on like this: Charlie, Delta, Echo, Foxtrot, Golf, Hotel, India, Juliet, Kilo, Lima, Mike, November, Oscar, Papa, Quebec, Romeo, Sierra, Tango, Uniform, Victor, Whisky, Xray, Yankee, Zulu. So if you're Agent J, you could be called Agent Juliet!

Other alphabet names

Imagine you start to call someone Agent E (her first or middle name could be Emily). You could change it using a suitable adjective, for example, Agent Elegant. Or you could choose an animal beginning with E – do you think she would she like to be called Agent Elephant?

Animal names

You can use plenty of other names – anything you like, really. Animal names work well, for example, Wolf, Tiger, Eagle, Snake, Panther, Python, Leopard or Fox. But you probably won't want to call your friends Agent Rat, Mouse, Tortoise, Guinea Pig or Dog!

Colourful character names

You can add colours to make interesting names, for example, Black Bat, Red Spider or Blue Falcon.

Number names

Famous spy James Bond was Agent 007. You could choose some interesting numbers for yourself and your friends, such as 111, 707 – or even 007½!

Codenames for operations

If you're planning an undercover operation, you'll need a codename for it. You could use a name that says what will happen, such as Operation Knockemdown or Operation Hidenseek, or you could choose a name that's the opposite of what you're planning, such as Operation Cuddles or Operation Neat and Tidy.

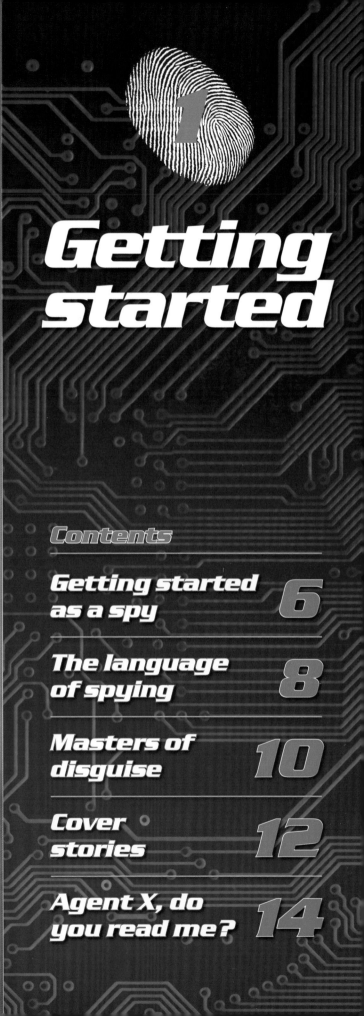

Getting started

Contents

The language of spying

There are special words for you to learn now you're entering the mysterious world of spying. Many of the words seem normal. Most people think they know what they mean. Read on, and find out what they really mean...

Spies often use special words.

Spies have many names, such as *spooks, crows, hoods* and *ghosts*. *Espionage* is a fancy word for spying. *Intelligence officers* is a fancy term for spies. *Intelligence* in the spy world means stuff that tells you something about the country or people you are spying on. An *intelligence agency* is an organisation that manages spies. The largest one in the world is the CIA, the USA's Central Intelligence Agency. There are two British ones – MI5 and MI6.

Follow that man!

Spies often follow people. That's called *trailing*. The person you're following is called the *target* or *quarry*. If you follow someone closely so they don't notice, as if you really are their shadow, that's called *shadowing* or *tailing*. A *tail* is a spy who's following someone else.

Surveillance means watching someone secretly, or keeping an eye on a building.

Discovered!

Your *ID – Identity* – is who you are. A false ID is a false identity – where you're pretending to be someone you're not. Sometimes spies have several different identities. It can get very confusing. Your *codename* is a name that hides your real name or is for a special operation

Someone you think may be an enemy spy is a *suspect*. A spy who is working in enemy territory in disguise is called an *undercover agent*.

Your *cover* is a story or ID you can use so people think you are someone else. If your *cover is blown* it means your enemies know who you are. Spies say you're *burned* – if you're caught when doing something; and you've *flown* – if you've left in a hurry.

Traitors!

Spies sometimes change sides. If you *turn around* a spy it means you get him to come over to your side. You might need *sugar*! That's what spies call a gift or money to persuade someone to help you.

And watch out for a *mole* – that's a baddy who's pretending to be one of your spies, or a goody who is pretending to be one of their spies. And be wide awake for a *sleeper* – that's a spy who is sent to live normally in a country for years, and then gets instructions to start his spying work.

A *double agent* is a spy who starts off working for one side then changes sides. His old friends still think he's working for them. If someone double-crosses a spy ring, it means they change sides. This could be when a double agent (who's pretending to be on their side but says he's working for you) then works for them again but pretends he isn't. Very confusing!

TAILING

themselves. They also send stuff that they know will be *intercepted* – picked up and read – by enemies! This information will be wrong on purpose, to mislead people. This is called *misinformation* – telling people things that give them the wrong ideas. You could leave a message saying you're meeting at RV1 when you're not, and all the baddies you know might go to the wrong place.

Pass it on!

A *drop* is somewhere you leave secret messages or information. A *DLB*, or *Dead Letter Box*, is where you leave messages without seeing the person collecting. A *letter box* is a person! It's someone who looks after secret documents for a spy to collect. A *contact* is someone an agent has to meet. You may need a special password before you can talk. You need to agree different *RVs* – *Rendezvous* – which are meeting places.

Spies don't only pass on messages for

Check your equipment is working before any mission

Spy jobs

A group of spies is usually called a spy ring. Members of a spy ring have different jobs.

Head of operations
In charge of everything and everybody.

Codemaster
In charge of making and decoding messages.

Scribbler
In charge of keeping notes of meetings and messages.

Security chief
In charge of everything to keep the spy ring free from danger, for example, making sure your house is safe and free from bugs.

Gadgets officer
Gets all the ingenious kit ready.

Supplies officer
Prepares all the food, drink and other things you need for a good trip.

Communications (Comms) officer
Makes sure you have the right satellite and phone links.

Field officer
Goes out into the field – this usually means going wherever your operations take you, into towns and cities (but if you have fields nearby they're good too!). Also sometimes recruits contacts.

Courier
Carries messages or other stuff for you. Not necessarily members of your spy ring. May not even know they're carrying things for you. (They don't even need to be human! Do you have a cat or dog that could be a courier for your spy ring?)

Masters of disguise

Spies often have to pretend to be someone else. Who would you like to be? Get a good disguise and a good cover story, and you'll confuse friends and enemies. Read on and learn how to make sure no one guesses who you really are!

Hats and scarves
These are very useful for hiding your face. It's a good idea to have several at the ready.

Moustaches
Face paint is good for pretend moustaches. You can also buy fake ones from joke shops. Although they are very useful, they can be a bit itchy. They may even fall off – a disaster on a dangerous assignment!

Glasses and sunglasses
Glasses and sunglasses make it harder to recognise people (that's why film stars and secret agents wear sunglasses so often).

Face paint
You can buy excellent face paints from many toy shops and craft shops, or you can use adult make-up.

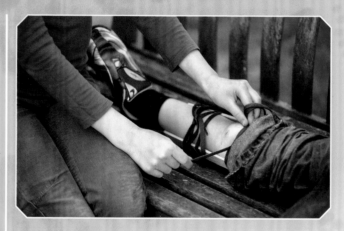

Stiff leg
Walking as though you have a wooden or stiff leg may put baddies off your scent. Take two rulers or two pieces of thin wood and some string, bandages or long laces. Tie the wood or rulers above and below your knee and you'll soon be walking as if you have a bad leg!

Walk with a limp
A simple way to do this is to put a stone in your shoe. It's not very comfortable, but it will trick people!

Hairsprays
Some hairsprays change the colour of your hair – a great disguise.

Wigs
These can be good for hiding your face as well as your hair.

Hairstyle
Change the way you wear your hair, for example, brush it up if you normally have it flat, wear pigtails if it normally hangs long.

Be someone else

When you use make-up or face paint, think how you can make your face look different from normal. For example, if you have dark eyebrows, use make-up to make them fair, and you'll look surprisingly different in a moment.

Agent D is having a spy make-over. He has a pale complexion so he's being given a darker one. He has fair eyebrows and is clean shaven. So he's been given dark eyebrows and stubble to show that he hasn't shaved for a couple of days. A good way of painting on stubble is to use the scouring side of a sponge scourer – dab black paint lightly.

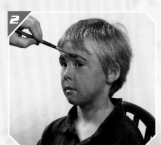

Agent F is planning to do some spying in a cold, foreign country. So he's going to look paler than normal. Black eyebrows and moustache show up his pale skin. With the glasses who would guess his real age?

Fine clothes, good make-up and glasses can make a young spy, like Agent C here, look much older.

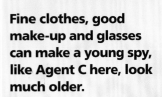

Paint on a scar and moustache: Agent C has become a dangerous-looking man!

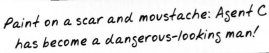

Cover stories

Spies often have to pretend to be somebody else. They do this partly by having a 'cover' or 'cover story', which hides their real identity. Every spy who doesn't want to be identified needs a foolproof cover story. You have to be able to say who you (now) are – and prove it!

Some of the best cover stories are those that stay close to the truth. So a 10-year-old from London shouldn't have a cover story that says he's a 16-year-old from Glasgow – unless he is very tall and very good at doing Scottish accents!

Spies may have different cover stories depending on who they are talking to. You want to be able to talk to people and answer their questions without looking suspicious. So, for example, if you know an area very well because you have been there often on holiday, saying you live there would be good for your cover story.

The table on the facing page will help you plan some details of your cover story. Copy it or write in the gaps on this chart.

What can you do with make-up and hair gel?

Getting ideas

Creating a disguise usually starts with applying make-up, but there are lots of other things you can do to help create the 'perfect disguise'.

These drawings from a spy book written over 100 years ago show how a person can look different by changing a few things.

Information	The truth	Prepare your cover	Cover story
My name is		Think of a different name	
I was born in		Think of somewhere else that you know	
I go to --- school		Think of another school near you	
I now live in		Think of somewhere else you know well	
I like to eat		Keep to the same, or you might be offered food you don't like	
I don't like to eat		Keep to the same	
I can speak (which languages)		Be honest!	
My mum's name is		Make it up	
My dad's name is		Make it up	
My parents' jobs are		Make them up	
My best friend's name is		Make it up – don't let enemies know their real name!	
My favourite colour is		Make it up (and remember it) or be honest	
My favourite football team or sports are		Pretend it's another team, and make sure you know all about it, or stick to your team	
My hobbies and interests are		Be honest so you can have a good chat!	

Agent X, do you read me?

'Do you read me' doesn't mean you have a book in your hands! It's a piece of 'open code' to check that someone can hear you.

Spies (and people such as pilots and the police) use many codewords and phrases. When spies talk on walkie talkies or a phone, they know that enemies may be listening in. Part of the conversation may be in open code, which is not secret, but understood by many people. Part of the conversation may need to be top secret, so spies invent special codewords and phrases.

In the table on the facing page are some codewords and phrases. The first ones are open code; the others can be the start of your secret language. You can make up more and more for you and your spy ring. You can use these secret phrases when you talk on walkie talkies, telephones and tin telephones. And some of the phrases could be handy when you are talking face to face, perhaps over a meal when you don't want friends or family to know what you're up to!

Cat in a basket!

Directions over the airwaves

Talking over the airwaves means using a phone or radio. This is the way spies, policemen and soldiers often give directions to others: they find a starting point and then give directions from there.

Look straight ahead of you. Imagine a clock. Straight ahead of you is called 12 o'clock. A little to your right is 1 o'clock, a little to your left is 11 o'clock. Do you get the idea? So where's 6 o'clock? Immediately behind you! Using the time on a clock is a very handy way of giving directions. Here's an example – you want to tell your spies to follow a suspect who has just walked past a park bench, to the right. If you say 'suspect at 3 o'clock, 50m from park bench' they'll soon find him.

'Target in view at 3 o'clock!'

Tin telephone

Make your own great communications! This is a good way of talking with friends. Young spies have been using these telephones for over 100 years. They may not be quite as good as regular telephones, but you don't need wires, electricity, credit or contracts. You can talk to people up to 100m away, if you have the string and the space.

1 You need a nail, a hammer, some string and two cans. Use the sort of cans that have ring pulls and leave no sharp edges. Wash them out thoroughly. Make a hole in the middle of both tins with the nail and hammer. You may need adult help. Cut the string to the length you want. Thread it through both holes. Put a knot on each end to go inside the can.

2 To use the tin telephone, you have to pull the string very tightly between the two tins. To talk, put your mouth right into the tin and speak loudly. To listen, put your ear into the tin.

Walkie talkie

Open code

Do you copy?............ Do you hear me OK?

Roger? .... Do you understand?

Roger....................... Yes, I understand

Roger so far? ....Have you got that bit?
(in the middle of
a long message)

Willco .... Will do it
(after an   (short for will
instruction)   cooperate)

May Day! May Day! .... Help!

Over. .... I've finished, you
                                can talk now

Out....................... End of conversation

Secret code

Big dog here!....... Aaargh! I am being tailed

Teatime 6................... Meet at 6 o'clock

Shut hospital! ....Cancel all operations!

Wait 2?.................. Are you OK to wait
                            for 2 minutes for
                            further instructions?

Back 10?..................... Can we talk in
                                   10 minutes?

Dragon flying low! ....Can't talk,
                                  mum's coming

Tarzan in trees! ...... Can't talk, dad's coming

Donkey in stable!.............. Can't talk, my
                               brother's listening

Cat in basket! .... Can't talk, my
                                 sister's listening

High-tech gear

Being a good spy doesn't have to stretch your pocket money too far. But if you did have loads of money, which of this high-tech gear would you buy? Prices range from £100 to £100,000,000!

▷ Spies use all manner of equipment to gather information – including spacecraft. This is a copy of a satellite called Grab I which was launched in 1960 to spy on Russian secret radar bases. Its mission was so secret that no one knew about the operation until 1998.

▷ Another way of collecting information sent by telephone (which often goes through space) or other methods using the sky and space, is by building an antenna farm like this one belonging to America's very secret Central Intelligence Agency (CIA).

The spy satellite Grab I

This watch doubles as a microphone

◁ This spy watch is the sort top agents like James Bond would wear! This particular one has lots of functions – including a microphone, a walkie talkie for keeping in contact with friends, and a tiny camera for taking photographs.

▷ Lots of secret organisations use spy cameras. This one belonged to the once feared East German Security Police called the Stasi.

The famous Lockheed U2

△ This is the most famous spy plane in the world – the Lockheed U2 ' Dragon Lady'. Because it flies on the edge of space taking photographs of secret bases, the pilot must wear a space suit – just like an astronaut!

◁ This is a secret pen microphone that plugs into a recorder.

▽ Spies have always used tiny cameras to take photographs of secret documents – just like this!

2

Spy's toolkit

Contents

The spy's toolkit

All good spies like to have special equipment. Some want simple things, some like complicated, technical gadgets; others like to have stuff that is disguised and looks innocent, so if they get stopped and their luggage is searched, no one will suspect anything. What would you like? Read on now to learn about and make some essential spy equipment...

Ⓐ Torch
Wise spies keep spare batteries in case the others run out.

Ⓑ Money
Cash is always handy. You might find it useful to collect coins from different countries so that you can buy a bus ticket wherever you go on an assignment!

Ⓒ Pens
Take normal pens and waterproof markers with you to write messages that won't wash away!

Ⓓ Paper and notebook
Keep at the ready for secret messages and making notes.

Ⓔ Weapons
You need to protect yourself. Spies use all kinds of weapons. You can make some of your own (see pages 20–25).

Ⓕ Stencils
Want to hide your handwriting? Or make coded messages really neat? Or make some official-looking notices? Stencils can be really useful...

Ⓖ MP3 player
Well, that's what it looks like, but it could be a radio receiver picking up sounds from a microphone miles away!

Ⓗ Sweets
These are important. Why? First, you may want to bribe your friends and enemies, getting them to do daring deeds, or to tell you vital secrets in exchange for some yummy sweets. Second, you may need to eat them yourself if you can't find any contacts to bribe – or if you're hungry!

Ⓘ Binoculars
Good for surveillance (watching people).

Ⓙ Sunglasses
To help your disguise and to stop people realising what you're looking at and what you're thinking!

Ⓚ Camera
During World War Two, spies often had small cameras which they could hide in their luggage or disguise as other things. Today, many 'normal' cameras are already very small, so people won't guess you're using them for spying operations.

Ⓛ Radio or mobile phone
Spies use all kinds of communications – methods of talking and sending messages. See page 14 to find out about making your conversation secret and safe!

Ⓜ Compass
If you're reading a map, you need to know which direction you're going in. It's important to know which way is which, and a compass tells you that. In World Wars One and Two, spies sometimes used tiny compasses, hidden in clever places such as hairbrushes, buttons or the heels of shoes.

Agent X

Make a pistol

Difficulty rating

Here's a small pistol to make that you can easily hide in your clothing, ready to protect yourself from sudden danger. Ask a friend to help if you can, because an extra pair of hands will come in useful.

PROJECT COMPONENTS

- ▶ Marker pen
- ▶ Scissors
- ▶ Thin cardboard
- ▶ Corrugated cardboard
- ▶ Ruler
- ▶ Five sheets of A4 paper (scrap pieces are OK)
- ▶ Masking tape

SEE CUTTING DIAGRAM ON PAGE 98

- ▶ Dowel rod, 6mm diameter x 15cm long, or a pen
- ▶ Glue
- ▶ Pen
- ▶ Silver and black (or brown) paint
- ▶ Weight, e.g. heavy books

1 Mark and cut out shapes A, B and C in thin cardboard to make templates. Draw round these shapes on the corrugated cardboard (note the direction of the lines on the diagram). You need to make two of shapes A and B per pistol. Using the edge of the scissors and a ruler, score the two A pieces as on the diagram. You need just one triangle shape C.

2 Fold four A4 sheets in half and cut into two pieces, to make eight A5 sheets. Keep together.

3 To make the pistol barrel, roll all the A5 sheets around the dowel rod or pen, then tape firmly with several pieces of masking tape (blue tape was used here so you can see what to do, but normal cream-coloured tape is fine). Push the rod or pen out. To make the handle, glue together the shapes, in the order A + B + B + A, making a kind of sandwich. Put a weight on the sandwich and leave to set.

4 Put the triangular sight guide C on the barrel, then glue and tape in place.

5 Bend back the card for the handle along the score lines and push it onto the barrel. Glue and fix with masking tape.

6 Cut a strip of paper about 3cm x 30cm, then roll it tight to make a plug for the end of the pistol. Glue into place.

7 Wrap some more masking tape around the handle to make the edges look smoother. Paint to finish.

Now you can make more guns! You can experiment with different shapes and sizes to build up a great collection. When you've had a bit of practice you can work out how to make longer barrels, and add silencers and telescopic sights, too. Make sure you have plenty of weapons for your spy ring!

Question

What kind of shoes do spies wear?

Answer

Sneakers

Sharpshooter gun

Difficulty rating 🔒 🔒 🔒 🔒 🔒

Danger! There are assassins on the roof tops! Can you stop them? Imagine you're on duty to protect some very important people (VIPs), and you've spotted someone suspicious. A gun like this will come in handy if you're a highly trained marksman who has been taught to shoot accurately – its long barrel will help you hit a target far away. And you can also easily hide this gun because it pulls apart and will fit into a small briefcase – or even a lunchbox!

PROJECT COMPONENTS

- 62 sheets of A4 paper (scrap or new sheets)
- Craft knife or scissors
- Marker pen
- Thin card
- Corrugated cardboard
- Strong paper glue (hot glue is perfect for this)

ADULT HELP NEEDED

- Weight, e.g. heavy books
- Dowel rod, approx 40cm long x 15mm diameter
- Masking tape
- Elastic bands
- Silver, grey or black paint

SEE CUTTING DIAGRAM ON PAGE 99

1 Count out four sets of 12 sheets of paper and put aside. Count out 12 sheets and cut them in half to make 24 A5 sheets. Take two more A4 sheets and cut them along their length into 3cm strips, so you'll have a set of 14 strips 3cm x 30cm.

2 With the marker pen, draw out and cut shapes A, B, C, D and E on some thin card. Use these as templates. Mark the shapes on corrugated cardboard – you need to cut out two of each shape. Write the letters on the pieces so that you don't get them mixed up. Pay attention to the lines of the corrugated cardboard on the diagram – make sure the lines are in the same direction on the pieces you cut.

3 Glue together pieces A + B + B + A to make a kind of sandwich. Make another sandwich with pieces C + D + D + C. Leave to dry under a weight.

4 Take one set of 12 sheets of paper and roll it *lengthways* round the dowel rod. Stick with tape and leave it on the rod. Take another set of 12 sheets. Roll this *widthways* around the set already on the rod.Tape it up and gently pull it off the lower set. Repeat this once. Now do it a third time but leave this roll on the dowel.

5 Take the set of smaller sheets you prepared in step 1 and roll it round the two sets of papers already on the rod. Pull them all off carefully. You now have three medium tubes, a longer, thinner one and a shorter, extra-thick one.

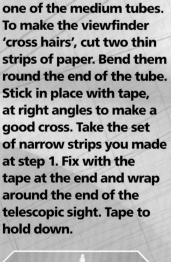

6 To make the telescopic sight take one of the medium tubes. To make the viewfinder 'cross hairs', cut two thin strips of paper. Bend them round the end of the tube. Stick in place with tape, at right angles to make a good cross. Take the set of narrow strips you made at step 1. Fix with the tape at the end and wrap around the end of the telescopic sight. Tape to hold down.

7 Insert and glue one of the three middle-sized tubes into the thickest one – put a lot of glue onto the thickest tube, and stick the telescopic sight on top. Try to get the sight's crosshairs as upright as possible. Use elastic bands to hold in place, and leave glue to set thoroughly.

8 Take the cardboard 'sandwiches' you made at step 3, bend back the card at the top and glue onto the gun body.

9 Bend the two strips E around your hand to make them flexible, then tape and glue around the gun. Glue the two bars F in place. Make a small roll of paper to plug the end of the gun and glue in place. Paint to finish, then fit the gun barrel back in.

Pea shooter

Pea shooters are just fun for kids to play with, right? Wrong! This isn't just fun. In the hands of cunning spies like Agent W here, they have several uses. You can shoot things at targets, you can send messages by shooting rolled-up paper, you can shoot poison darts, you can spy on people and you can give out an alarm call. What will you try first?

PROJECT COMPONENTS

▶ A4 sheet of paper
▶ A 5p piece
▶ Masking tape or Sellotape
▶ Paints and paintbrush

AMMUNITION!

▶ What ammunition do you want to fire? Try these: dried chick peas, small balls of dampened tissues, tin foil rolled into small balls, peanuts and round sweets like mint imperials (which shoot brilliantly if you don't mind not eating them!).

3 Tape down the paper roll. To paint the peashooter so that it will be difficult to spot (or camouflage it), paint along the barrel mixing red and green. Leave about 1cm bare at one end, where you will be blowing.

1 Roll the sheet of paper along its width. Roll it loosely once, then roll again tighter.

2 Now roll it to about the same diameter as a 5p piece. Use the coin as a guide.

Three-in-one tool

Peep down it like a telescope! You'll find it helps you see things more sharply. You can peep through curtains or bushes. Spot people when you're in a car or on a bus.

Ready, fire! This is the most important use: this cool peashooter will fire all sorts of ammunition.

Poop poop! Sound the alarm! This is also a sonic signalling device. It takes practice – unless you already know how to get notes out of a trumpet. You have to 'blow a raspberry' into the tube, and when you have got it right, it will play a loud note. This note can be a signal for your contacts. It can carry a long way. Baddies will find it difficult to work out where the sound is coming from.

Target practice

You need a target to help you improve your accuracy. This one is easy to make.

PROJECT COMPONENTS

▶ An empty large yoghurt pot

▶ Thin cardboard from a cereal packet

▶ Scissors

▶ PVA glue or Sellotape

▶ Marker pen

▶ Masking tape

▶ Paper

▶ Wooden kebab skewers

Shooting

You can get good results by simply blowing with a 'whoosh' ; but you can get even better results using another method. Put your lip into the tube, not around it. Put the tip of your tongue over the end of the peashooter. Start to blow. Make a kind of tutting action with your tongue: this gives a stronger blast of air.

NEVER shoot at people's faces. Don't use hard ammunition such as small stones.

Practise shooting quite close up first, then move further away

'Poison' darts

1 Cut the wooden kebab skewers into 10cm lengths. Cut some rectangles of paper, 2cm x 4cm.

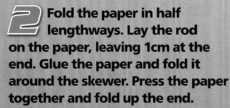

2 Fold the paper in half lengthways. Lay the rod on the paper, leaving 1cm at the end. Glue the paper and fold it around the skewer. Press the paper together and fold up the end.

3 Take a 5cm length of masking tape and wrap it round the other end. You're ready to fire the dart. If the folded end is too large for your peashooter, trim it at the corners. If the the dart doesn't fly straight, you may need to add some more tape to the end.

Colour in to make the darts look deadly!

1 Cut the edge off the cereal packet and open up the sheet. Draw round the top of the yoghurt pot to make a circle on one side.

2 Now draw another circle inside the first one, about 1cm from the line of the first circle.

3 Cut out this smaller circle.

4 Make little cuts all the way round between the small and the large circles, about 1cm apart.

5 The yoghurt pot should now fit snugly into place.

6 Cut out a cardboard strip and glue or tape it to the two sides of the target to help it stand up. Decorate the target if you like. Now start peashooting!

Super bugs

A bug is the name for a tiny microphone that spies hide in rooms and other places, when they need to listen in on conversations. The bug picks up the conversations and transmits (sends) them to a radio receiver so that the spymaster can listen in. Bugs can be hidden in many things such as a pen, watch or piece of jewellery. People who are good at electronics can make bugs that really work. But if you're not into electronics – and don't have enough pocket money for a real bug – it's no problem. Make some of these bugs instead. They look really good and are as easy to hide as the real ones.

PROJECT COMPONENTS

- ▶ Marker pen
- ▶ Polystyrene sheet (or you can use the base of pizza packaging or fish-and-chip boxes)
- ▶ Waterproof markers (dark colours)
- ▶ Drawing pins
- ▶ Blu-Tack

Some watches contain hidden bugs

Moving bugs

Sometimes spies wear a bug on their clothes to record a conversation with a contact. Imagine you're meeting a top spy at a café near you. You could stick a bug on your shoe, on a belt, in a pocket or under a large watch. Where would you put one? Or you could put one in a car – how many places can you think of to hide a bug there?

Hiding bugs

You can stick bugs around your house to surprise your family! Hide them where they won't be noticed. The best places are often below eye level. This is because things below eye level are usually less noticeable than things above eye level. Here are some really good hiding places:

▷ on a bookcase
▷ under a shelf, table, bench or chair
▷ on the base of a lamp (don't put it close to a bulb) or the edge of a picture frame.

You also need to be sure that the bug is placed somewhere that is suitable for recording, as if it was a real one, so, for example, under a pillow isn't a good place because the sound will be muffled.

1 To make the bugs, draw several rectangles on the polystyrene about 1cm x 2cm and cut them out. Draw squiggles on each rectangle with the waterproof markers to look like camouflage. This will make the bugs harder to spot. Push a drawing pin into the edge of each bug.

2 Put small pieces of Blu-Tack onto the bottom of each bug. Now you're ready to hide your bugs. Stick them in places where they can't be seen easily.

Agent X has chosen a good hiding place under a mantelpiece

Spy sweep

This game tests how skilled you are at hiding and finding bugs. You'll need to make 13 bugs to play.

1 Divide into two teams, A and B, with up to four people on each team.

2 Team A starts by hiding all the bugs around the room you're playing in while Team B waits outside.

3 When Team A is ready, Team B enters the room and does a sweep searching for the bugs. When they have found all the bugs, or have given up looking, gather the bugs together.

4 Now it's Team B's turn to hide the bugs and Team A has to look for them.

5 The team that finds the most bugs is the winner. Another way to decide on the winner is to time how long it takes each team to find all the bugs. The fastest team wins.

Special cars for spies

Sometimes spies need a normal car that no one notices, sometimes they need a really smart one. And sometimes they need one with ingenious gadgets. One of the most famous spies is James Bond. He has driven the most amazing cars, with an incredible array of gadgets and weapons. Here are some of them. Imagine – what gadgets would you add if you had your own special car? Why not copy one of these cars and draw in the gadgets you'd choose?

Goldfinger
Aston Martin DB5

What makes this car special?

- **Get lost!** Shoves other cars away with front and rear rams.
- **Tat, tat, tat!** Machine-guns behind the front indicator lights.
- **Down you go!** Slashes enemies' tyres with knives at the sides that go in and out.
- **Brr...brr. 'Are you there?'** Radio phone hidden in the door.
- **I can see you!** Radar scanner on the wing mirror and a tracking screen on the dashboard show where enemies are.
- **Bye-bye!** Passenger ejector seat – a piece of the roof flies off before the seat shoots out!

The name's Martin, Aston Martin

- **Squidge!** Oil squirted from rear lights to cause skidding.
- **What a let-down!** Bursts enemies' tyres with 'calthrops' – nasty triple-pointed nails that shoot out from the rear lights.
- **Now you see me, now you don't!** Blinds enemies with smoke-screen cartridges that drop out from the exhaust pipes.
- **Guns at the ready!** Arms store under driver's seat.
- **Can't shoot me!** Bullet-proof front and rear windscreens.

The Spy Who Loved Me
Lotus Esprit

What makes this car special?

▷ Mud sprayers at the back squirt mud over chasing cars.
▷ Goes underwater – the car becomes a submarine.
▷ Blows up helicopters with surface-to-air missiles.
▷ Sinks ships with depth charges (underwater bombs) and torpedoes (underwater missiles).
▷ Blinds the enemy with underwater smoke screens.

Undercover and underwater

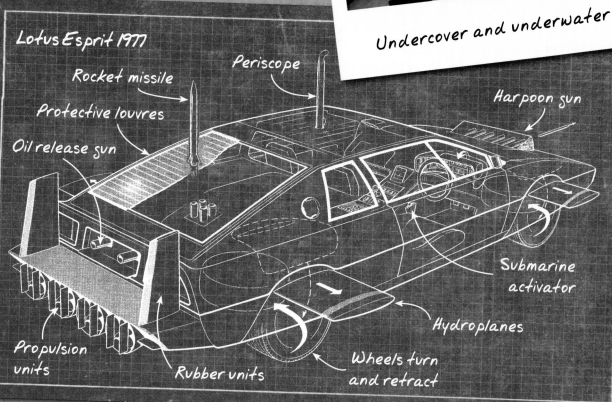

Lotus Esprit 1977
Rocket missile
Periscope
Protective louvres
Harpoon gun
Oil release gun
Submarine activator
Hydroplanes
Propulsion units
Rubber units
Wheels turn and retract

Die Another Day
Aston Martin V12 Vanquish

What makes this car special?

▷ Looks can kill! Has rockets and machine guns that come through the front grille.
▷ A really smart car! Uses special guns under the bonnet that sense movement and go off automatically.
▷ Keeps its cool! Drives on ice with special spiky tyres.
▷ Disappears! Just switch to invisibility and your enemies can't see you. How cool is that!

KE02 EWW

Codes to trick your enemies

Spies love codes. You can use them to hide messages in many clever ways. All you have to do is tell your friends how to decode the message, so they'll understand it. How to decode is often called the key to a code. Make sure your enemies don't discover the key!

Different secrets

Today most of us simply call it a code when we put anything into a secret language. Spies know that, to be exact, you can change words with codes and ciphers, which are different.

Codes

A code is when you replace a message with words or letters that still seem to make sense, for example, 'I'm going to see Agent J' could be changed through a code (encoded) into 'I'm cooking sausages'! A code creates a new message that looks normal but is actually hiding a secret waiting to be decoded.

Ciphers

A cipher is different, because what you end up with doesn't seem to make any sense. For example, one cipher simply involves writing each word backwards. So 'help' is changed (encrypted) into 'pleh'. Getting it to make sense again is called 'decrypting'. Some ciphers replace letters with numbers or special signs.

Now you know the difference, you can show off to other people! But in everyday language, we usually use the word 'code' to include both ciphers and codes. Whichever method you use, keep your secrets safe and be sure to confuse the enemy!

Today, a spy can carry a computer this powerful in his pocket!

Hard to crack

It can take great computing power to break the most top-secret messages. This machine was built during World War Two. It was called 'Bombe'. Top mathematicians and engineers from Britain, Poland and the United States designed and built it. It helped the allied forces understand messages sent out from machines like Enigma, on the right.

Enigma

This is the famous World War Two German 'Enigma' machine. It sent out secret messages to German soldiers all over the world. But British codebreakers, based at a top-secret building called Bletchley Park, eventually cracked the Enigma by using the world's first electronic computer called 'Colossus'.

3

Cool codes

Contents

Silent speaking

Imagine. You're in a room with your contact in sight. You need to get a message across but you must be sure no one sees or hears it. What do you do? Or you've discovered your enemies have laid a trap in a shopping centre. You must warn your contact, but can't be seen talking to him. What do you do?

The answer is to use body codes – movements that mean things. Here are some body codes for you to use and you can also make up some of your own. Until you become expert at this, keep your code simple or you'll get confused. Your job is to look perfectly normal – don't make any of your movements look odd or people will notice. For example, don't have a code that requires you to wink lots of times – that's very suspicious.

Movement
Shut both eyes as if blinking but for longer than normal

Meaning
Yes, understood

Movement
Scratch one ear in the middle

Meaning
Please repeat. I missed that or didn't understand

Movement
Wipe eye with hand

Meaning
No

Movement
Rub chin

Meaning
I don't agree

Movement
Rub both eyes

Meaning
Danger. Mission aborted. Leave immediately

Movement
Touch nose with one finger

Meaning
Meet me at RV1 (rendezvous or meeting place) in a few minutes

SPY
Manual

Movement
Lick lips

Meaning
Bring food

Movement
Both hands on table

Meaning
Leave stuff at our dead letter box

Movement
Touch ear lobe

Meaning
I'll phone you

Movement
Head resting on one hand, two fingers up

Meaning
Shall we get our bikes?

Movement
Brush a bit of hair back

Meaning
Go back home

Movement
Head resting on one hand, three fingers up

Meaning
Let's go and find Agent C

Movement
Arms crossed

Meaning
I think we're being watched

Movement
Touch cheek with one, two, three or four fingers

Meaning
You decide – time to build up your own code...

What's Agent W trying to tell us here?

Answers: 1. Go back home; 2. Bring food; 3. Meet at RV1; 4. Shall we get our bikes?

Outdoor signals

If you're outdoors the signals shown on the previous page might be too obvious. You can work out a set of signals for when you're walking, standing, or sitting on a bench. You can invent secret signals just for walking past your contact – nobody will notice! Here are some signs you can use...

Movement
Arms crossed, legs uncrossed

Meaning
Danger! I think we're being watched. Don't approach me but walk on and I'll follow

Movement
Touch side with three fingers

Meaning
Meet at RV3 in a few minutes

Movement
Scratch back over shoulder

Meaning
Wait and follow me

Movement
One hand in pocket, one out

Meaning
Follow me to a safer spot

Movement
Arms crossed, legs crossed

Meaning
Danger! Proceed with caution: we are not alone

Movement
Touch side with four fingers

Meaning
You decide – time to build up your own code...

Morse code

Morse code was invented by Samuel Morse in 1844 and for more than 150 years it's been used by soldiers, sailors and spies. Morse code works by turning each letter in the alphabet into a series of dots and dashes, or long or short signals.

How to send in Morse code

If you want to send and receive messages in Morse code, write out your message in dots and dashes. Practise with short messages at first and allow long gaps between words when you do the signalling. If you can, work in two pairs: one pair sends the message, with one using the code table and telling the other what to signal. It helps to count in your head. A dash should be about as long as three dots. So 'A', which is 'dot dash', count as 'dot dash-two-three'. Between each letter allow a gap that is equal to three dots; between two words, allow a gap equal to about five dots.

The pair receiving the message needs one person saying what he sees and the other one writing it down in dots and dashes – they can decode it later.

> You can send your signal by ringing it on a doorbell; tapping it out with your fingers or whistling it; or you could flash it with lights, using a Morse-code signaller or a Spy CD (see next page).

Morse alphabet

A	•—	J	•———	S	•••	2	••———
B	—•••	K	—•—	T	—	3	•••——
C	—•—•	L	•—••	U	••—	4	••••—
D	—••	M	——	V	•••—	5	•••••
E	•	N	—•	W	•——	6	—••••
F	••—•	O	———	X	—••—	7	——•••
G	——•	P	•——•	Y	—•——	8	———••
H	••••	Q	——•—	Z	——••	9	————•
I	••	R	•—•	1	•————	0	—————

SOS ••• ——— •••

Morse code signaller

ADULT HELP NEEDED

Difficulty rating 🔒 🔒 🔒 🔒 🔒

When it's getting dark, it's a good time to send some Morse-code signals to friends who can see the windows of your home. But flashing signals can often be tricky with torches because you can't always switch them on and off quickly enough. This piece of equipment will help you to signal better.

PROJECT COMPONENTS

- ▶ Ruler and set square
- ▶ Pencil
- ▶ Knife or scissors
- ▶ Corrugated cardboard
- ▶ Glue
- ▶ Newspaper
- ▶ Weight, e.g. heavy books

SEE CUTTING DIAGRAM ON PAGE 100

MORSE CODE

1 Using a ruler and set square, measure carefully, then cut out all the pieces of cardboard and mark them with their letters. You may need some adult help. Pieces A, F and H have a diamond shape. Draw a 4cm square on some paper or card, cut it out and use as a template. Follow the diagram to get the right position, and draw round the template.

2 Glue pieces B, C, D and E onto piece A. Note: there is a 5.5cm gap between D and E.

3 Fold piece G (the handle) around the right-hand end of piece F and glue. Piece F is going to be sandwiched between pieces A and H. Lay piece F on piece A, but do *not* glue as it needs to move. Check that it can slide along easily – if not, trim a few millimetres off the top.

4 Glue the top of pieces B, C, D and E and place piece H on top of them, taking care that no glue touches piece F in the middle of the 'sandwich'.

5 Fold piece J around the left-hand side of the assembled pieces and glue. Put some newspaper on top and underneath, and then some heavy books on top to weigh the cardboard down. Leave the glue to dry, for at least an hour.

6 To start signalling, put your torch by the opening of the signaller. You can rest it on a book to raise it to a better height or perhaps have an assistant to help you. Pull the handle backwards and forwards to flash on and off quickly.

Spy CD code

How do you catch someone's attention in a flash? People have been using mirrors for signalling for hundreds of years. You can use an old CD and keep it at the ready – no one would guess what it's there for!

You need a sunny day. Hold the CD so that it puts a blob of light near or onto the face of the person you want to contact. They'll soon see you. If your spy friends have a CD at the ready, they can flash back to confirm they've seen you.

You can send various messages. You can use the CD to send Morse code (see page 37), or you can agree on a simpler code with your friends. For example, two flashes could mean 'meet back at your home', three flashes could mean 'meet back at my home' and four flashes could mean 'meet at the park'. Once you get the hang of it, work out codes for much more complicated messages!

WARNING: Always wear sunglasses in bright sunlight, as the signals can easily dazzle you and might damage your eyes.

Grid code

Some codes replace each letter with a number. Here, you use a grid or table to tell you the right numbers. It's easy for you to put words into code — but very difficult for enemies to crack the message!

PROJECT COMPONENTS

► Two sheets of A4 paper, plus extra paper for decoding the message

► Two different-coloured pens

Double dealing

Using playing cards like this to send secret messages has always been a favourite ploy of spies. If you're allowed to ruin a few playing cards, see if you can pull the layers of the cardboard apart. You can try soaking the card first, or get adult help and a very sharp craft knife. You can hide thin things in the card, or write messages, and glue it again if you like.

You'd never spot this code in a pack of cards

1 To make your grid of eight rows of eight rectangles, fold each sheet of paper in half, then half again, and then half again once more. Open up the paper and press it flat. Now fold in the other direction as before. Open up the paper and press it flat.

2 Leaving the four corner rectangles blank, with one pen write numbers 1 to 6 along the top and bottom rows, and 1 to 6 down both sides. Now with the other coloured pen, write all the letters of the alphabet, plus numbers 1 to 9, in any order scattered all over the place, one in any box. When you have finished, there will be one blank rectangle which you leave empty.

3 Copy your grid onto the second sheet. Carefully check that you have the letters and numbers in exactly the same places. Now you're ready to encode some messages. Your friend will need the second sheet to decode your messages and send you some, too.

How to do grid references

Each letter or number will have what's called a grid reference. It consists of two numbers. Choose your letter. What horizontal (across) row is it in? That's the first number of the grid reference. What vertical (up) row is it in? That's the second number of the grid reference. Always write the horizontal number first, and the vertical number second. Here is a good way to remember which is which. Imagine you're going to climb a ladder – you walk *across* to it first before you climb *up* it!

If you look at the grid, 'spy', for example, becomes 15 (1 across, 5 down); 35 (3 across, 5 down); 21 (2 across, 1 down). So now you can write any message replacing every letter with a two-number code. Can you crack this message?

34, 13, 14, 42, 16, 23

15, 42, 16, 31

26, 25, 13, 42

33, 46, 25, 33, 25, 51, 22, 23, 42

What has Agent G written?

Muddling maths messages

Now you can prepare some messages to write down and send to your contact. You could even email them. And to be really cunning, you could disguise your message as if it was maths homework. This looks like three innocent sums – but it's actually a message in disguise! What does it say?

31	23	66
25	42	25
16	51	15
23	51	46
──	──	──

Now you see it, now you don't

You can make invisible ink from many things. All spies have their favourites. There are three main types of invisible ink. First, there are pens with special ink which becomes visible under special lights. Secondly, there are certain chemicals that look invisible but appear when mixed with other particular chemicals. And thirdly, there is a group of invisible inks that is easy to get and use, and is really effective – this type becomes invisible as it drys but reappears with heat. This type you can easily use yourself.

PROJECT COMPONENTS

- Dip pen or alternative
- Paper
- Milk or lemon juice
- Greaseproof paper
- Iron

ADULT HELP NEEDED

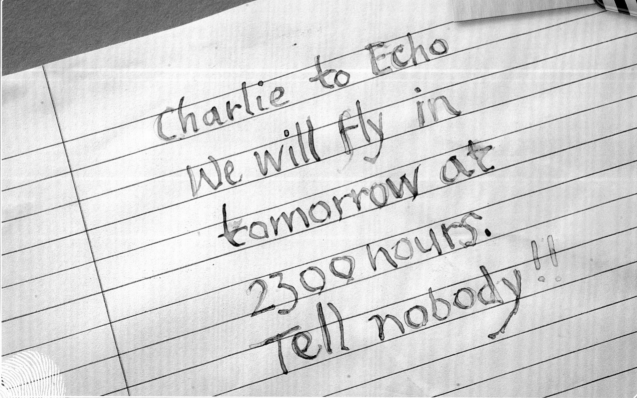

Several liquids that you probably have in your kitchen make very good invisible inks. Which would you like to try first? Do you have some lemon juice or milk? These are the best to use, but you can also use orange juice, onion juice, vinegar or sugar solution (sugar dissolved in water).

If possible, find an old-style dip pen for writing your secret messages. You can also use a fine brush to write with or a very tightly rolled piece of paper as a sort of stick pen. A cocktail stick or barbecue skewer will work, too.

1 Write your message on the paper, dipping your pen into the liquid often to make sure there is plenty of invisible ink on the paper. Leave to dry thoroughly. Send the  message to your contact, who will need to have greaseproof paper and an iron ready, and help from an adult.

2 To reveal the message, lay greaseproof paper over the paper with the message. Switch on an iron  to maximum heat. Lay it on top of the greaseproof paper for 2 minutes. Peep at the message. If you can't see it yet, place the iron on top of the greaseproof paper for another 2 minutes.

3 Instead of using an iron, you can also make your message visible in the following ways. Ask an adult to help you.

▷ Put the paper into a medium-to-hot oven and check every 5 minutes.

▷ Pass the paper over a hot light bulb (be careful not to touch the bulb as it could burn you).

▷ Wave the paper gently over a candle flame. You need to take care, so get a grown-up to help you. Keep the paper a little above the candle flame, moving slowly back and forth. Make sure that it doesn't burn – you don't want your precious message to go up in flames!

Code red

This is another cool way to hide messages, maps and diagrams.

1 Write your secret message on some paper using light-green and blue pens only. Leave a large gap, about 1cm, between each letter.

2 Using orange, pink or yellow pens only, write extra letters in the spaces, to muddle up the message. You can choose any letter. If you're drawing a map or diagram, add lots of squiggles and lines so that you can't spot the thing you first drew. You now have a page that is *very* confusing!

3 Here comes the magic bit. Send your message to your contact, who will need a transparent, red, plastic sheet. They simply place it over your work – the muddle will disappear and the message will be clear again!

Computer messages

Here are three clever ways of hiding messages using a computer. You may need to ask for some adult help the first time you do these tricks. The instructions here are for Microsoft Word. You may need to use different computer commands with other word-processing programs.

Spies sometimes use special cameras to make microdots. These are dots about 1mm in diameter that carry tiny messages and diagrams. To read them, you need to use a special microscope. You can make very tiny messages on your computer, rather like microdots.

1 Open up a word-processing program such as Microsoft Word – check first that your contact's computer has the same program. Type a decoy message. This is a message that has nothing to do with your secret message. As it's perfectly visible, your enemies won't realise there is a hidden message as well. Make the decoy story three or four lines long and reasonably large – use 12–14pt type. Divide it into two or three paragraphs and make the first message realistic to fool the enemy.

2 In between the paragraphs start a new line for your secret message. First type a few capital 'Xs' and '0s'. Now start your secret message, typing in capitals. At the end add more capital 'Xs' and '0s'. Don't worry if your message goes over onto two or three lines.

3 Now for the cunning bit! Select all the 'Xs' and '0s' and your secret message. Change the size to 2pt. How do you do this? If you have a font-size button on your toolbar, click on the down arrow to the right, type 2, then press Enter. If you don't have a font-size button, click on Format, then font size, type 2 and press Enter. This will make your message almost invisible.

4 You can email this micro message to your friend as an attached file (ask your mum or dad to help you). When he receives it, all he has to do is select all and change the font size back to 12pt or 14pt, and your message will reappear! (To change the font size back, click Select All with your mouse or click Edit then Select All, then follow the instructions at stage 3, but this time choose 12pt or 14pt.)

Micro messages printed out

Here you make micro messages in exactly the same way and print them out. Write a decoy message first of all, then write your secret message. Select the secret message and change its size to 3pt [see stage 3 on page 44]. When you print out your document, you'll have some really tiny writing that needs a magnifying glass if you want to read it. The photo shows the writing a little larger so you can see it better.

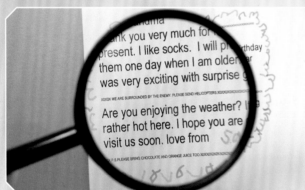

Disappearing messages

Here's another brilliant way of hiding a message in a computer document to send to another spy.

1 Write your decoy message and then write your secret message.

2 Select the lines of the secret message. If there is an A on your toolbar with a colour underneath, and another button to the right with a downward arrow, click that. Then click on the white box. (If you don't have it on the toolbar, click on Format, then Font, then Colour and click the little white box.) Now your message has disappeared, because it's white on a white background.

3 Email the document to your friend. Tell him how to find the message – all he has to do is select the whole document, click on Colour, and choose black – and hey presto, your message will reappear!

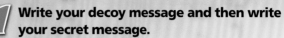

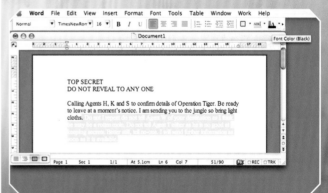

Easy cool codes for hot secrets

Reverse writing

Write every word backwards, for example 'spy' becomes 'Yps'. 'Please come to my party' becomes 'Esaelp emoc ot ym ytrap'.

What does this mean?
(Answer at the bottom of the page.)

Gnirb stol fo steews.

Shift one

With this code, you change each letter to become the next one in the alphabet. For example: 'a' becomes 'b'; 's' becomes 't'. So 'spy' becomes 'tqz'; 'Please come quickly!' becomes 'Qmfbtf dpnf rvjdlmz!'

What does this mean?
(Answer at the bottom of the page.)

Hfu up nz ipnf cz 4 p'dmpdl.

Mysterious markings!

Most people think signposts simply give directions to places. But spies have secret signposts which provide important information.

Spies don't necessarily leave signposts in particularly secret places. They may be where they can be easily spotted, although most people will probably walk straight past them. Even if they notice the signs, people aren't likely to give them a moment's thought. That's the really clever thing about spy signposts. Other people can't 'read' them – but you can! Your spy ring has to decide what signs to use and what they mean. Here are some examples:

▷ One thing on the signpost means 'go to meeting place 1'.
▷ Two things the same means 'go to meeting place 2'.
▷ Three things the same means 'go back to headquarters'.
▷ Three things – two the same, one different – means 'come back tomorrow'.
▷ Four things – two the same, two different – means danger, 'run away'.
▷ Twigs in the shape of an arrow means go to 'meeting point 1 immediately'.

Signpost quiz
(answers at the bottom of the next page)

1 Agent E leaves a signpost of three round stones at someone's door. What does this mean?

2 Agent E has found a deliberately broken twig with two breaks. What does this mean?

3 Agent C has placed three twigs at the foot of a tree. What does this mean?

4 Agents E and C have found a signpost of two flowers in two different colours. Looks pretty – but what does it mean?

5 Agent C has prepared a signpost to put where only the car driver will see it. If you look carefully, she has used two types of knot, an overhand knot and a figure of eight knot. So what's the message?

Mark this well

You can use chalk to leave secret marks in many places. Can you see any? Agents E and C are walking past without stopping, so no one will notice. But they're paying attention. Here's what the marks mean. Each line represents the time – one line is 1 o'clock, two lines are 2 o'clock, a line across is half an hour. Here are three lines, and one across, meaning meet at 3.30.

Answers: 1. Go back to headquarters; 2. Go to meeting place 2; 3. Go back to headquarters; 4. Danger! Run away; 5. Danger! Come back tomorrow.

Handling secrets

Contents

Swish switches

If you want to give a fellow spy something, you don't want your enemies spotting you. So what can you do to pass vital secrets to a contact without anyone seeing? Do a switch! Usually you switch two things that look the same. You can do a switch using small items like newspapers, pens and glasses cases, or larger things like coats or cases. Switching things needs practice but you can soon get really good at it.

Bag switch

You need two bags that are the same. It could be two lunchboxes or two shopping bags with about the same amount of stuff in them. In the photos here, the two lunchboxes have different colours, so that you can see clearly what's going on.

1 Agent S sits at a bench and puts his lunchbox a little way from him.

2 Agent H strolls across, puts down his lunchbox and sits down, too.

3 After a while Agent S casually picks up Agent H's lunchbox, and walks away.

4 Agent H goes off with Agent S's lunchbox. What secrets or treasure have they exchanged?

Newspaper pass

A pass like this is similar to a switch, except that the agents don't swap things. One agent keeps everything. Look at what's happening in the photos.

1 Agent J is reading on the bench.

2 Agent M approaches, sits down and also reads. They don't talk.

3 Agent J leaves his magazine on the bench.

4 A few minutes later, Agent M picks it up with his own magazine and leaves.

Left luggage

This is another way of secretly passing material. Instead of swapping two items, there's only one which is collected by your contact. For example, you leave a book or magazine lying on the bench with secret stuff inside, and your contact takes it when no one is looking.

1 Agent S puts a backpack under a bench.

2 He reads for a while then goes away, leaving the backpack.

3 Agent H arrives on his scooter.

4 Picks up the bag and leaves straight away.

Parachute drop

Difficulty rating 🔒 🔒 🔒 🔓 🔓

Do you want to send something important to one of your spies in another country – or the garden next door? One way to do this is to send a plane and drop stuff by parachute.

PROJECT COMPONENTS

▶ Plastic bin bag

▶ Large dinner plate

▶ Waterproof marker

▶ Scissors

▶ Thread

▶ Sellotape

▶ Two sheets of A4 paper

Some pigeons received medals for their good work

Dropping in

In the First World War, the British intelligence services even sent carrier pigeons into enemy territory by parachute. They asked French people to help with information about what the German army was doing. The information went into special pouches attached to the pigeons and they sent the pigeons flying home. Over 500,000 pigeons were sent. Some of them even carried cameras.

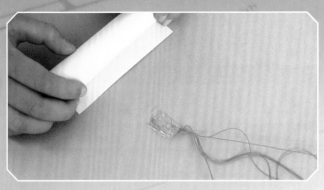

1 To make the parachute, place the bin bag under the dinner plate and draw round it with the marker. Cut out the circle.

4 To make the carrier, roll and tape a piece of paper. Fix it with tape to the tape that is holding the threads together. Write your message. Roll up your message and slip it into the carrier. You're ready for the launch!

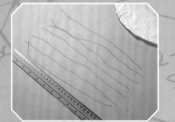

2 Cut eight pieces of thread about 30cm long. Fix one thread 1cm inside the edge with Sellotape. Fix another thread on the opposite side. Imagine the first was at 12 o'clock. The next one is a 6 o'clock. Repeat at 9 o'clock and 3 o'clock, and then in between so that you have all eight threads attached and evenly spaced. Gather together all the loose ends onto a 3cm piece of Sellotape. Fold the tape so the sticky side is pressed onto itself.

5 To send the parachute, drop it from somewhere high such as from the top of the stairs, or by standing on a chair or ladder. It's good to throw it from an upstairs window, but the parachute may get caught on something, especially if it's windy. This parachute is too small to carry much weight but it can take messages and a silk map if you have one. If you want it to carry heavier items such as a code book or even an Action Man-type toy, cut a parachute with a 70cm diameter.

3 Draw a 1cm square in the middle of the parachute. Cut it out (this will help it float better).

Super spy glider

Difficulty rating 🔒🔒🔒

Spies have often used gliders to send messages, information or supplies. They fly silently and can be hidden from radar tracking. This is a great paper glider which also flies silently and is even more unlikely to be picked up by enemy radar. It can carry a message from you to your contact.

PROJECT COMPONENTS

▶ A4 sheet of paper

▶ Sellotape or masking tape

SEE CUTTING DIAGRAM ON PAGE 98

1 Fold the paper in half both ways. Open it up flat. With the larger side on top, fold the bottom up to the middle. Fold again, bottom edge up to the middle. Turn the bottom section up over the middle crease (see diagram) so that this crease becomes the bottom edge. Fold the paper in half widthways with the folded section on the outside.

3 Get your secret message ready. Cut a piece of paper about 3cm x 3cm then fold in half (the photo shows you where it goes – tuck it in completely).

4 Test the plane. It should glide in the air – just like an eagle. For the best flights, let go of it gently (rather than throwing it hard). Let it fly from a height – for example, while standing on a chair or from an upstairs window. You may need to experiment to improve the flight, changing the angle of the wings if necessary.

2 Make folds at the bottom, about 2cm on either side. Make folds on the wings about 2cm from the edge. Use Sellotape or masking tape to fix the front and the back body and wing edges.

Silk maps

It's often important to get things really small if you want to hide away secrets. Paper maps are quite bulky when you fold them up. Spies solved that problem long ago by writing or drawing on silk. Silk is a soft material that squashes down to almost nothing! (Magicians also use large silk handkerchiefs which they can easily squeeze into tiny places.)

1 Pin or tape the cloth onto some corrugated card to hold it in place. Draw a real or pretend map.

2 When the map is finished, you can squish it into the carrier of a parachute (see page 51) or hide it away in other small containers.

Hiding secret messages

The best places for hiding things depend on what you're hiding and where you are. How clever are you at hiding things? Sometimes you'll find good hiding places that are already perfect to use. Sometimes you'll need to make something specially. Here are loads of ideas for hiding things.

Twigs and logs

If you live near woods or parks, you'll find plenty of good hiding places there. You can hide messages in the cracks of large logs or you can drill holes in thick twigs and branches. Get adult help for this. Ask them to drill a hole with a thin drill bit first and then drill again with a thicker one as that works best. Then you can roll up a message and pop it in so no one will spot it!

There are lots of good hideaways

Roll up and pop in your secrets!

Secrets down under

You can easily place messages under things where they won't be seen, for example, a watering can or a flowerpot. Just remember to tell your fellow spies where the message is, as they'll never find it otherwise!

On a car

You can often slip a message under the back numberplate of a car or place it behind one of the mirrors.

People don't notice things right in front of them!

Undercover with underwear

Does anyone hang up any washing at home? Put a message on a peg, and no one will notice it. Just make sure your contact picks up the message before anyone takes down the washing!

By a building

Ivy grows up buildings in many places. Is there some near you that would provide a perfect hiding place? Are there any drainpipes near you? Put messages behind them and nobody will spot them!

In a park or garden

If you have a garden or park nearby, large leaves will come in useful. Here's why. Find a pair of large leaves. Lay one on top of the other and staple together, leaving a gap so that you can put your secret message inside. Put the leaves on the ground. Would anybody notice them?

Tasty hiding places

Here's another challenge! How can you get urgent messages up to one of your contacts in a hotel? Agents F, D and T worked on the problem. Here's how they solved it.

1 Don't get burnt! Cut the toast in half. Slit the toast down the middle to make a pocket and slip the message inside.

2 Tea spells trouble! Send a message written with a waterproof marker on a piece of plastic bag. Drop it in the tea but be careful if it's hot.

3 Safety warning in your cereal! Can you hide messages in your cereal?

4 Look behind you? No, look underneath! Folding paper this way is called a concertina fold. The paper takes up very little space when folded.

5 Sweet surprise! It's easy to hide small folded messages in a bowl of sugar – who'd guess this was there?

Dead letter boxes

When you have lots of secrets in your pocket, you often can't give them directly to your spy ring, as enemies might spot you. So what do you do? You might use a dead letter box (DLB). A DLB is a place where you can leave things for someone to collect. (It's called a dead drop because you pick up the things when no one is there. It is different from a 'live' drop, when there's someone to receive things or pass them over to another person.)

You can set up a DLB in all kinds of places. If you have a short message to leave, you'll only need a small DLB. If you have a load of secret information, you might need a big hole in the garden. Just as you may have several RVs (rendezvous or meeting places), you may want several DLBs. Your spy ring needs to know where they all are. You can tell a contact to go to a particular one or check them all. Make sure you can get to your DLBs fairly easily, but don't choose places where other people will immediately spot them.

Ready signals

Spies usually leave signals about when to collect from dead letter boxes. You wouldn't want to go to one if it wasn't ready. Usually spies use three signals when making a drop. They are not left too close to the DLB – and could even be miles away. The signals show the following:

▷ Ready to be filled – you must wait.
▷ Ready to be picked up – you can collect now.
▷ Emptied – I've picked up the material (from the spy who collects the information).

You might prefer blue

Think pink

In the 1960s, John Vassall worked in the Admiralty in London – but he was also a KGB agent spying for Moscow. It was too dangerous to telephone his Russian boss to arrange a meeting, so he would draw a pink circle on a tree! Spies often use different signals to pass messages to one another. You don't even have to talk as long as you understand what certain things mean – just like the ones shown on the facing page.

Hiding places in the house

Agents L and Y had an assignment to find hiding places for messages in their home and had some neat ideas. What hiding places would you use?

1 Pop it in a pepper!
Food in your kitchen can provide tasty hiding places. You can make pockets in pitta bread or hide messages in bananas! Can you think of other hiding places?

2 Anyone for a nightcap?
Do you like cocoa or drinking chocolate? Inside the tin's a good place to hide a hot message!

3 A picture's worth a thousand words
That's a well-known saying. And spies know that there's enough space behind and in picture frames to hide a thousand words – though it would be best if your message was a little shorter!

4 Fancy an interesting read?
With spies about, even boring books can get exciting! Slip a message into a book, and no one will notice. Just remember to tell your contact which book and which page, or they'll have a lot of reading…

Which signals will you use? There are lots to choose from and there are loads of ideas on pages 46 and 47. Here are two.

Crosses
Using traffic lights is one idea. At your signal point, leave a small piece of paper with a red cross on it. Then, when the DLB is ready, draw an orange cross below it. Your contact draws a green cross below the orange one when he's finished.

Stones
Choose three stones, and put them next to each other. When the DLB is filled, take one away and your contact can remove the last one when he's taken the information.

Spy challenge
Some of the hiding places on pages 54 and 55 would make good dead letter boxes. When you choose a DLB, you need to be able to get to it fairly easily, but don't choose places where other people will easily spot it. Can you think of three things you'd like to pass to your contacts in a dead letter box? And which two places near where you live would make secure DLBs – one for something large and one for something small?

Chamber of secrets

ADULT HELP NEEDED

Difficulty rating 🔒 🔒 🔒 🔒 🔒

Agent E takes out a normal-looking book — but it's not normal at all! It has a hidden chamber with a matchbox in it. And what's in the matchbox? Just a few diamonds and pearls! Here's a cunning way of hiding valuables and secret information.

PROJECT COMPONENTS

- ▶ Thick book (no longer needed) with at least 200 pages, plus some other heavy books for weights
- ▶ Matchbox
- ▶ Marker pen
- ▶ Craft knife
- ▶ Metal ruler

- ▶ PVA glue
- ▶ Piece of greaseproof, wax paper or foil a little larger than the book

Hide your valuables and secrets here

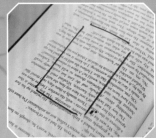

1 Take the book and turn to about page 51. Place the matchbox in the middle of the page and draw round it with the marker pen.

2 This job needs two pairs of hands. Ask an adult to use a very sharp craft knife and metal ruler to cut through the pages a few millimetres wider than the rectangle on

each side. You will need to hold the side of the book up – to be cut neatly, it should not rest on the table. Ask your helper to cut through enough pages to make a hole a little deeper than the thickness of the matchbox, so that it will fit snugly inside the hole without being seen.

3 Put plenty of glue inside the chamber, spreading it along the edges with your finger. Wash your hands well when you have finished.

4 Lay the greaseproof paper on top of the chamber to stop the pages sticking together. Weigh down with the other books and leave to dry overnight. Now you have a book that looks like any other book – except that it has a secret hiding place!

Magic matchbox

It's useful to be able to hide small things away. Do you need a safe place for any miniature film, pearls or diamonds? Well, they'll be safer in this matchbox. You'll really surprise people with it! It can make things disappear before their eyes. You'll need a small box of matches, paper and Sellotape.

1 Empty the matchbox and put six matches to one side. Put the others away somewhere safe. On the paper, use the marker pen to draw round the outside of the inner tray of the matchbox. Cut out a rectangle, just a little smaller than your outline.

2 Lay the rectangle of paper so that one edge rests on the top of the cover and the remainder lies on the bottom of the tray. Use a small piece of Sellotape to hold the paper at the top, and another piece of Sellotape to hold the paper on the bottom of the tray.

3 Put your jewels or other valuables on the right-hand side of the box. Now, if you push the tray in and bring it out to the left – abracadabra – your valuables will disappear as if by magic, and you will only see the matches! Push back the other way and the valuables reappear. WARNING Never strike a match!

Message in a shoe

Your shoes make excellent hiding places. And you can make them even better. No one will ever guess there's anything sinister afoot!

PROJECT COMPONENTS

▶ **Paper**

▶ **Marker pen**

▶ **Shoe**

▶ **Scissors**

Library secrets

You want to avoid being caught with incriminating evidence – that means stuff that shows you're a spy. One way of doing this is to leave it somewhere else. Is there a public library near you? A favourite trick used by spies of old to pass information to friends was by inserting messages and photographs into books and leaving them in a library. Whoever was collecting the book had to time it right just in case the book was taken by somebody else.

Interesting what you find in books

1 On the paper draw round your shoe with the marker pen. On the paper draw a second line that follows the same shape but is about 1cm smaller all the way round inside the first shape. Cut this shape out.

2 You now have a new inner sole for your shoe – put it inside your shoe and slip your secret message underneath. Now you can step out with your secrets safe!

Hiding things on yourself

Where can you hide things on yourself where no one will see them? Here are three ideas.

Spies like to keep things under their hat!

Spy challenge

Can you find four good hiding places on yourself?

False-bottom boot box

Difficulty rating

A clever spy needs to have many hiding places. You can conceal important things in boxes that have a false bottom. This provides a brilliant, secret place underneath what looks like the regular bottom of an ordinary box. Here's how to put a false bottom in a shoe or boot box.

PROJECT COMPONENTS

- ▶ Shoe box
- ▶ Ruler
- ▶ Set square
- ▶ Knife or scissors
- ▶ Corrugated cardboard
- ▶ Glue
- ▶ Sellotape or masking tape

FALSE BOTTOM

1 Measure the length and width of the shoe box. Using the ruler and set square, cut eight pieces of corrugated cardboard 2cm wide. Four of the pieces should be half a centimetre shorter than the width of the box, and the other four pieces should be half a centimetre shorter than the length of the box. Cut one rectangle the same width and length of the box. This piece needs to really fit snugly. If it is too tight, trim a very little bit off one or two sides, so that the sheet fits well.

2 Gluing one piece at a time, stick each piece of cut cardboard inside the box at the bottom. Stick two layers on each side.

3 Make a little tab to lift the false bottom (masking tape has been used in the photos so that you can see it, but you can use Sellotape, which will be almost invisible). Take a piece of Sellotape about 6cm long and fold it in half so it sticks to itself. Stick another piece of Sellotape about 3cm long to hold it in place on the false bottom. To lift the false bottom and get to your hidden treasures, pull on the tab. Now you've got a box that looks normal. Who would guess it has a secret hiding place?

Card-holder

You can hide banknotes and messages in this cunning card-holder. It looks just like a simple wallet, but it has two secret compartments.

1 Fold an A4 sheet of thin card or paper lengthways and cut along the fold. Take one piece and fold it in half widthways. Open up. Fold from the sides into the middle fold.

2 Put a thin line of glue along the top and bottom edges of the paper. Fold up and press down. Place the card-holder on some paper, put a piece of scrap paper on top, then put several books on top to flatten it well. Leave until the glue is dry.

What message will you hide in your card?

Now you can write boring things on your finished card-holder to avoid people getting interested. To get to the secret compartments, bend the card-holder back so that the inside fold is outwards. Press from both edges and your two secret pockets open. No one will ever guess there's something hidden inside.

Camouflage cover

How can you make something very hard to spot? Try using camouflage. Something is camouflaged when its colour or pattern is similar to its surroundings. Many animals use camouflage to hide from enemies because they are able to blend in with the background. You can use it to conceal things.

PROJECT COMPONENTS

▶ Newspaper
▶ Marker pen
▶ Thin card, e.g. from a cereal packet
▶ Scissors
▶ PVA glue
▶ Trowel or old spoon
▶ Gravel

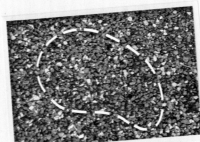

CAMOUFLAGE

Here's something that is so well camouflaged it almost disappears! You can hide secret messages under it – and unless someone knows where it is they are very unlikely to spot it, no matter how hard they search. This camouflaged cover uses gravel, because it's quite easy to find. If you don't have gravel on the ground near where you live, you can make one with other materials such as sand, general dirt or bits of wood. Get some advice from your parents before doing so.

1 Draw a blobby shape on the card and cut it out.

2 Squirt a lot of PVA glue on the card shape. Allow the glue to spread, making sure the whole shape is covered. This is a messy activity so put lots of newspaper down first.

3 Using a trowel or old spoon, gradually pour plenty of gravel onto the glue and press down lightly. Leave the glue to dry for at least 24 hours in a warm place.

4 Place your camouflaged cover on a driveway with a message under it, and you will see how it's amazingly hard to spot!

You wouldn't spot this man 100 metres away

Camouflage in the field

Many agents who work in dangerous areas often use camouflage to help make them difficult to spot. Sometimes that means wearing materials that are coloured like the woods and countryside around them, and patterned so that you cannot see their shape clearly.

Who's been here then?

Look at the pads of your fingers with a magnifying glass, or just with your eyes, very closely. Can you see whirly patterns? Fingerprints come from these tiny patterns. Because our fingers are very slightly greasy, they leave their patterns on the surfaces we touch, although they are hard to see.

No two people have the same fingerprint pattern, so it is a useful way to identify people. The police keep records of criminals' fingerprints, so when a crime has been committed, detectives will look for fingerprints and try to match them to those on their records. Spies who go snooping around looking for information will often wear gloves to avoid leaving their fingerprints behind.

It's very hard to compare fingerprints. The differences can be tiny. Today, experts who examine crimes use computers to make many checks in order to identify someone's fingerprints. There's no way you can change or disguise your fingerprints – even if you cut your finger the same patterns return. The only way you can lose your fingerprints is to cut your finger off!

Finding, collecting and saving prints are quite difficult tasks. Here are some secrets that will help.

Finding fingerprints

Fingerprints aren't very easy to spot – they're most obvious on shiny and dark surfaces. Where will you find some in your home? Walk around with a magnifying glass and see what you can find on, for example, used drinking glasses; cups and plates; photos in frames; used cutlery; sunglasses; smooth, dark metal and plastic surfaces.

Making fingerprints easy to see

One way of making clear fingerprints is to take a piece of Sellotape and press it between finger and thumb. Take it away and look very carefully at the Sellotape. The glue side should have a very clear fingerprint for you to examine.

Another way is to blow warm, damp breath onto your finger. Press it immediately onto a glass or smooth, plastic surface. If that doesn't work the first time, try again, first wiping your finger on the side of your nose, or in your hair.

FINGERPRINT

Fingerprints

Arch

Loop

Central loop

Double loop

Accidental

Lateral loop

Tented arch

Whorl

Everyone has their own fingerprints but forensic scientists have worked out that they can all be sorted into just a few types. Each person's fingerprints will follow one of these patterns. Have a good look here. Now look at your family's fingerprints very carefully with a magnifying glass. Can you match them to any of the patterns here? Now look for some fingerprints around your home and examine them very carefully. Can you work out who they belong to?

5

Watch out!

Contents

Fingerprint fun

You can become an expert at finding, revealing and recognising fingerprints. It takes a little practice and patience, and then you'll soon see some great results and can start making a special collection in your secret files.

Reveal a secret

Fingerprints are hard to see. There may be fingerprints hidden on a surface, even if you can't see them with your magnifying glass. You need to 'develop' them, or reveal them, with powder. Experts use very special fine powders but you can make do with powder found in your home. You can use either light-coloured powders, such as flour or talcum powder, or dark powders, such as cocoa or powder from a pencil (scrape the pencil lead with a knife or sandpaper, carefully keeping the powder on a piece of paper).

1 Agent C has been drinking from a glass.

2 Will her finger-prints show up? A dark powder will reveal them best. Drop a little cocoa on the glass. Gently blow the powder off.

3 Yes, her prints are clearly visible.

Capturing prints

When people have been arrested, they sometimes have their fingerprints taken. A policeman puts their fingers on a special inky pad, then presses them firmly onto a paper pad. You can take fingerprints in the same way if you have an inky stamp pad at home.

1 Press your finger firmly on the ink pad, then roll it from side to side but don't move your finger across.

2 Now press your finger firmly onto some paper. Again, roll your finger from side to side but don't allow it to slide across the paper.

3 If you've made a clear enough print, you can cut it out and stick it in a notebook. Perhaps you can find other suspects who will give you their fingerprints! Don't forget to write down whose prints are whose.

Tea-bag trick!

If you don't have a stamp pad, here's a special spy trick using tea bags.

1 You'll need a brush, paint and a teabag. Mix paint with water so that it's like thin cream.

2 Put the tea bag on a plate and brush some ink or paint onto it. Leave it for a few minutes to soak it up. Now your tea bag is ready to help you make prints in the same way the ink pad did.

Question
Why are mummies so good at being secret agents?

Answer
They always keep things under wraps

Cocoa-coated prints

Salami solution!

Normally, fingerprints on paper are very difficult to develop. This method will help you make good clear prints for your collection – and you can hide some of your equipment afterwards by eating it!

1 You will need some salami or cheddar cheese. Wash your hands thoroughly. Press one or more fingers lightly onto the salami or cheese. Press your fingers firmly onto the paper. Make sure they don't slip over the surface.

2 Drop a very small amount of cocoa over the paper. Shake gently and blow away the loose cocoa to reveal your fingerprints.

Look behind you

ADULT HELP NEEDED

Difficulty rating 🔒 🔒 🔒 🔒 🔒

Have you ever heard someone say they'd like 'eyes at the back of their head' to watch out for things? Here's the answer. Spies can have eyes at the back of their head – with the help of a trick mirror hidden in a book!

PROJECT COMPONENTS

▶ Small, flat mirror (or a small piece of mirror glass, available from a glazier)
▶ Old book that's no longer needed (check with mum first)
▶ Marker pen
▶ Duct tape
▶ Very sharp craft knife
▶ PVA glue

1 If you're using a piece of mirror glass (about 10cm x 7cm), carefully cover each edge with duct tape, taking care not to cut yourself.

2 Lay the mirror in the middle of the book and draw round it with your marker pen. Ask an adult helper to cut out through about 30 pages, using a sharp craft knife, until the mirror fits nicely into the space. Glue a few of these pages together at the front. Put more tape around the back of the mirror.

3 Now you're ready to watch the world behind you. Sit on a bench, hold the book up as if you are reading it and look into the mirror!

Daily spy

Here's a great way of spying on people and they'd never know! Turn an old newspaper into a spy paper.

1 Measure the distance between your agent's eyes and add about 5cm. Turn the newspaper to the last page but one. Mark out a rectangle about as wide as you measured, by about 3cm deep. Cut out the rectangle on the back two pages.

Large newspapers can be easier to spy behind

2 Now you have a newspaper that looks normal. You can pretend to read it and look at the pictures – and then whenever you want to spy on your target, simply turn to the back two pages!

Periscope peeping

Difficulty rating 🔒 🔒 🔒 🔒 🔒

A periscope is a clever invention that helps you spy on people. Periscopes help you to look around walls, corners and other obstacles without your target noticing. Submarines have periscopes so that sailors inside can see what is happening on the surface of the water when the ship is below the waves. Spies find periscopes very useful for spying.

PROJECT COMPONENTS

- ▶ Two small mirrors about 6cm high – the width slightly narrower than the cartons
- ▶ Duct tape
- ▶ Two juice cartons (1–1.5l)
- ▶ Thin cardboard from a cereal packet
- ▶ Scissors or craft knife
- ▶ Marker pen

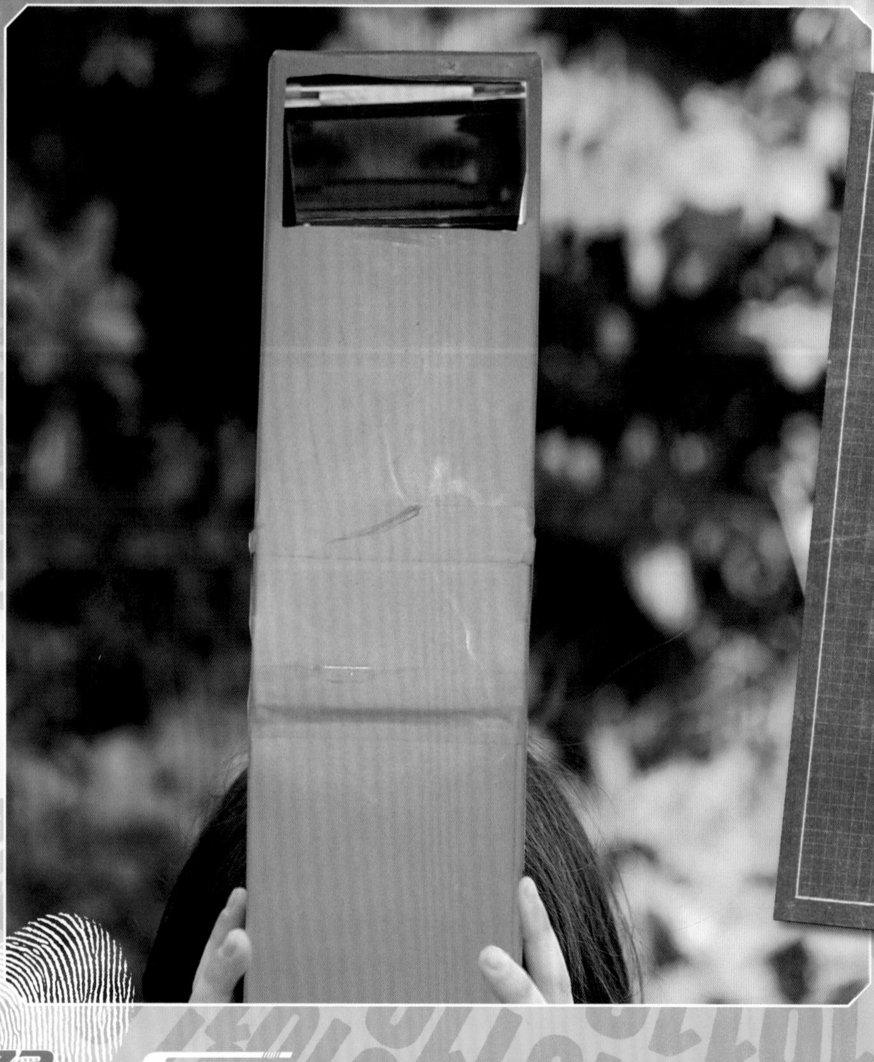

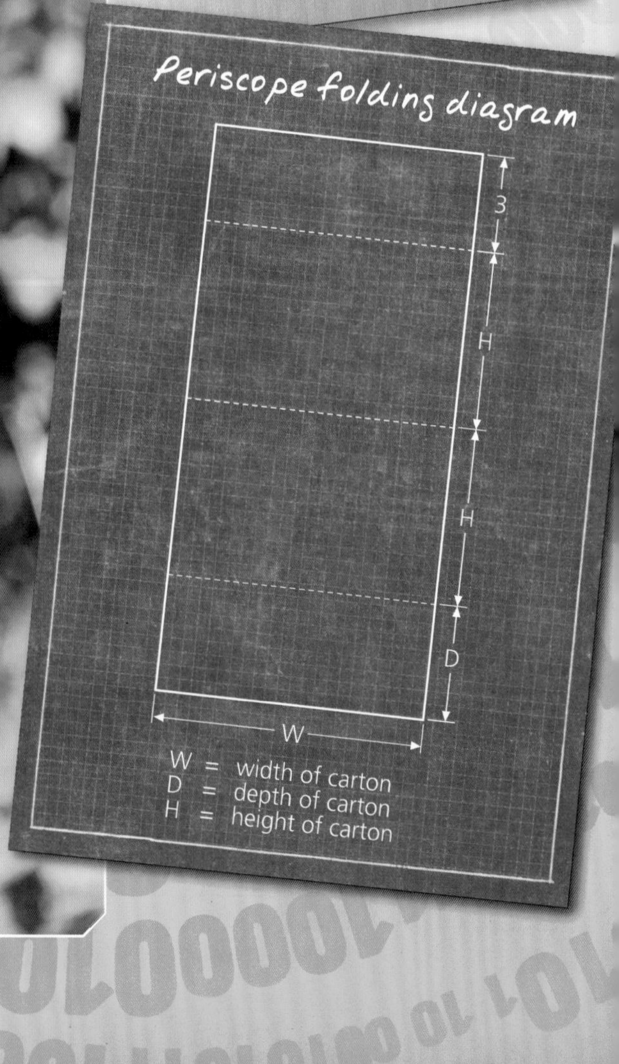

Periscope folding diagram

3

H

H

D

W

W = width of carton
D = depth of carton
H = height of carton

1 Getting the right size mirrors may be tricky. If they're difficult to find, get two cut at your local glazier. If your mirrors have sharp edges, carefully put duct tape on each edge.

4 Mark and cut the two pieces of cardboard (see diagram) – fold and tape them.

2 Remove the top of each juice carton. Cut a 3cm slit down each corner. Now cut a rectangle in the cardboard 5cm high and 1cm narrower than the carton. Use this rectangle as a template to mark rectangles at the bottom of each carton.

5 Use duct tape to fix the two mirrors into the two cardboard holders. Place each mirror into a carton and tape in place at the bottom. Slot the two cartons together between the slits, and fix with duct tape.

3 Cut out each rectangle from each carton to make two windows.

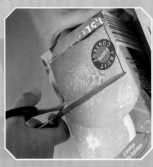

6 You can leave the periscope looking like juice cartons as a good disguise, or paint it. Spray paint works best: ask for adult help.

Paper project

Difficulty rating

Here's a challenge you can set up for one of your friends. It gives you an idea how a spy or detective would look very carefully at important evidence. The challenge is to see if your friend can spot the differences between very similar things.

PROJECT COMPONENTS

- Four pieces of different sorts of white paper (e.g. newspaper, writing paper, different thicknesses of computer printer paper, a magazine page)
- Pen or pencil
- A4 sheet of paper
- Scissors
- Strong magnifying glass

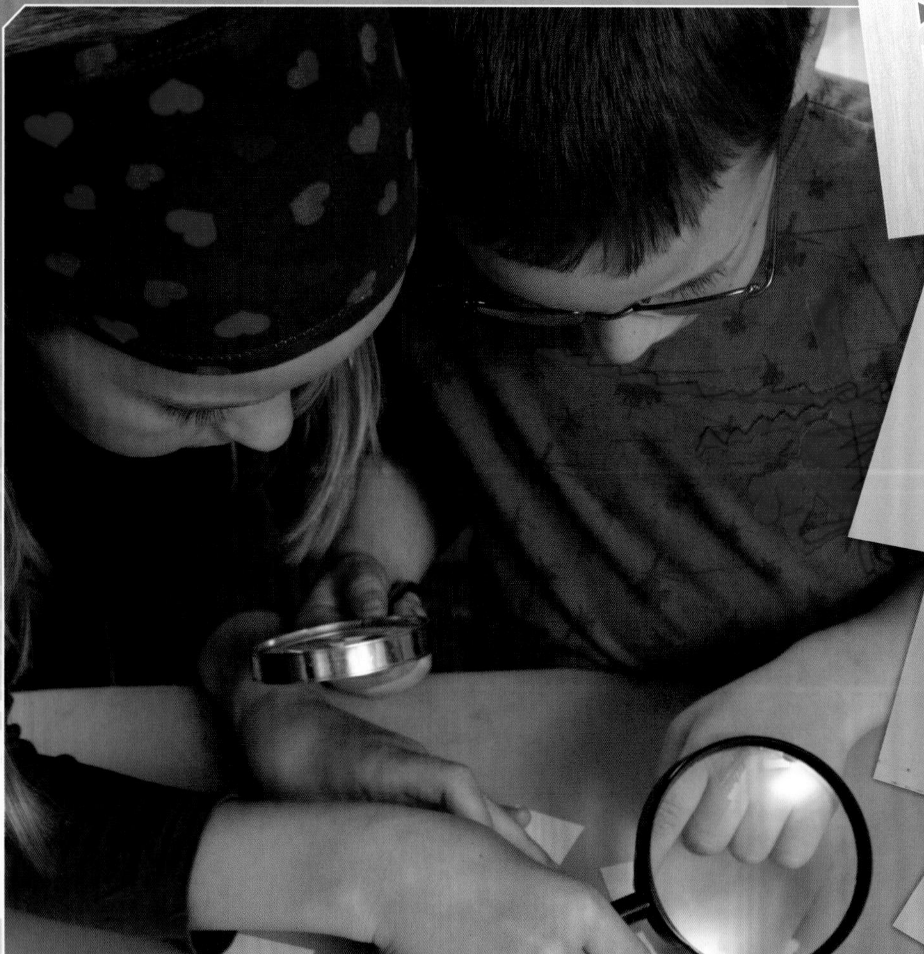

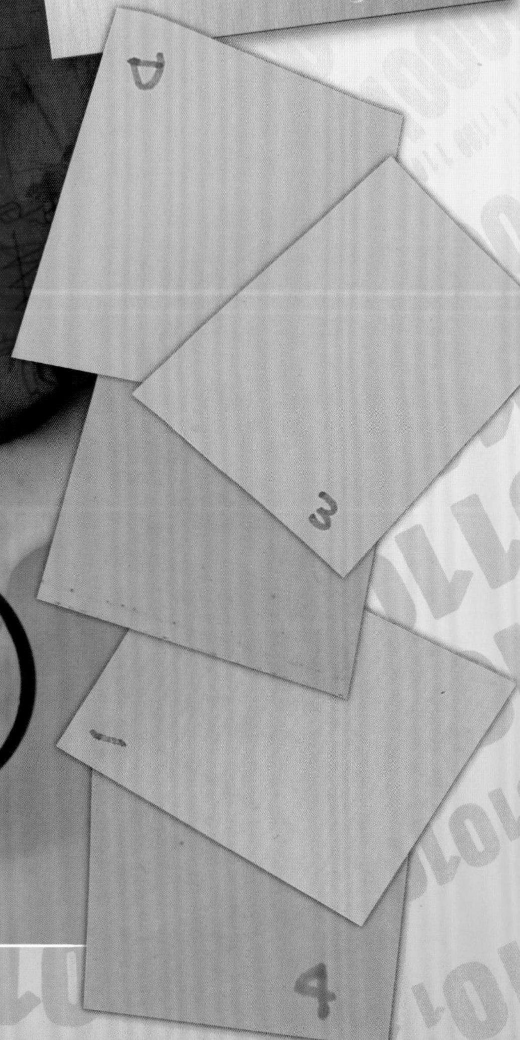

1 On the A4 sheet of paper, make a list of the papers like this, leaving spaces to be filled in.

Paper A	piece numbers _____ and _____
Paper B	piece numbers _____ and _____
Paper C	piece numbers _____ and _____
Paper D	piece numbers _____ and _____

2 Take the first piece of paper. Cut two rectangles from the side of the sheet. Write a number on each piece – any number from 1–10. Write those two numbers on your list. Repeat this for the other three types of paper, using different numbers.

3 Mix up and lay the pieces on a table. Give them to your friend and challenge him or her to match each piece of paper.

▶ **Surface:** look very carefully with the magnifying glass. See if there's any pattern. Is it shiny or quite smooth or rough? Hold the paper at an angle to the light so that the surface can be seen more clearly.

▶ **Colour:** many white papers are slightly different shades of white. Look carefully at what really matches.

▶ **Thickness or flexibility:** papers vary in their floppiness. Two papers that look very much alike can be quite different in this test.

▶ **How does it tear?** Different papers sometimes tear differently. Tear the sample paper slightly and look at the tear with your magnifying glass. You may see tiny pieces called fibres. Different papers often have different-looking fibres.

When your friend has finished, check the list to see if he matched the paper correctly. (You can now ask your friend to set a paper challenge for you, finding some other papers.)

Observing and learning

Keep your eyes wide open! Get your brain in gear here! A good spy needs to watch things carefully and work out what they mean. You can gather a lot of information from watching people and things carefully. The pieces of information you pick up are called observations.

Try keeping members of your family under surveillance (observation) for an hour, and see what you can learn about their daily habits – but make sure they don't realise you're watching them!

From your careful observations, you can work out other things – this is called 'deduction'. For example, if you see someone leaving the house in the morning in school uniform … what can you deduce? Or you see a long, fair hair on an armchair. What can you deduce from that?

Spies and detectives often work in similar ways, trying to solve mysteries or crimes by thinking very

OBSERVING

hard about observations, and making deductions. Sometimes it's easy to make good deductions. Sometimes you need more information before you can make a 'safe' deduction (i.e., one that's likely to be correct). Sometimes good deductions can suddenly be wrong when more information comes in. Two things are vital. You need to learn to be very observant, looking closely at details. And you'll need to learn how to watch carefully without being noticed.

Challenging coins

Some coins carry important clues. What can you find out with a magnifying glass? Study things carefully and make your own deductions...

PROJECT COMPONENTS

▶ Five 2p pieces – some shiny, some dull
▶ Magnifying glass

Heads, tails or spies?

Check your change

Spies use all manner of objects to hide secret messages – including coins! This particular coin was given to a young paper boy called Jimmy in New York in 1953. When he dropped it on the floor the coin opened up and inside was a secret set of coded numbers. After Jimmy handed it to the FBI, it led police to a gang of Russian spies.

Which is oldest

If you look at a coin with a magnifying glass, you'll see tiny scratches and dents. The pattern on a coin also often gets rubbed and smoothed out. Test yourself – can you judge the age of coins?

1 Lay the 2p pieces on a table, tails side up. Look very carefully at them. Look for scratches and nicks, and at how smooth, new and sharp the design looks. From your observations, which do you think is the oldest?

2 Now put the coins in order of age, starting with the oldest one on the left. Turn the coins over and look at the dates. Did your observations lead to correct deductions?

Observations and deductions

Spies, forensic scientists (who work with the police looking at evidence) and other detectives have to work on many types of information. When you look at something carefully, you begin to collect information. From that information you may get other clues. From looking at a battered coin, for example, you may think it's old. That's a deduction. It may be correct or it may be incorrect. You need further information to see if you're correct. With a coin, that's usually easy as there's probably a date on it. And that's usually reliable. But not always: what if the coin is lying?

The one on the right is a fake

Fake money

Counterfeit money means fake money. The police are very interested in finding the criminals who mount counterfeiting operations.

▷ **Colour:** Do you see the dark colour of some of the metal? This fake is plated, which means it has a covering of shiny metal and a different dull colour of cheap (or base) metal on the inside.
▷ **Soft metal:** A real £1 coin normally doesn't get dents and scratches this badly.
▷ **Design:** Although it was a good copy, now the design is wearing badly and looks unclear. Genuine coins are more precise and their designs are well defined. Can you see how the dots round the edge are very unclear on the fake?
▷ **Edge:** The pattern on the edge is rough because the metal is weak.
▷ **Weight:** A genuine £1 coin weighs exactly 10g. Some fakes are lighter and machines such as parking meters or ticket machines will reject them.

Some enemy spies and criminals print counterfeit notes, although they're very hard to fake. Look at a £5, £10 or £20 note under a magnifying glass. You'll see that the print is very fine, delicately coloured and very complicated. Some crooks make fake £1 coins. How can you tell?

Can you trust this contact?

Imagine you've been sent to meet a contact. How do you know you've met the right person?

Spies often need to meet up with people they've never seen before. So how do they check it's the right person? How can they be sure that it's safe to talk? Secret handshakes can be the answer. They tell you you've met the right person.

What's a spy handshake? It can be several different things. First, sometimes spies shake hands in a way that appears normal but is unusual. For example, you might tuck your third and fourth fingers back. You'd feel that but people wouldn't notice. Can you think of different ways to shake hands with people?

There are other 'handshakes' that don't involve shaking hands but are ways of telling you you're talking to the right person.

Codeword handshakes

To make sure you're meeting the right person, you and your contact need to learn some codewords or phrases to be used like a password. You say something, then the other person replies with an answer you're expecting. These codewords will help you check that you're meeting the right person and that it's safe for both of you to talk. You can make up your own codes. Choose some phrases that sound normal and decide what they really mean. You also need to decide what the opening sentence and reply should be. Here are some examples:

Agent A:

'That's a cool bike'

(this is what Agent B is waiting to hear)

Agent B:

'I prefer walking'

(this is what Agent A is waiting to hear)

Matching pair handshakes

Here's another way you can both be sure you can trust the other person: use matching pairs. Each person has one half of something that matches the other half exactly. Here are three examples. Imagine that Agents L and Y have never met before, but they've been given matching pairs to prove to one another they are who they are.

Money matches

Agents L and Y confirm their identity with their pieces of a £5 note that has been cut in half. Banknotes have unique (special to them) numbers on them. Have a look at one. If the numbers match, each piece must be from the same banknote.

Made-up money

Your parents may not be very pleased if you start cutting up their banknotes! So Agents L and Y have made their own spy banknote for other meetings.

Card match

Agent L cut up a playing card and sent it to Agent Y. As the pieces fit perfectly, they can prove one another's identities.

Coded conversations

Spies often use plain codes, where a sentence or phrase replaces another one. The coded phrase sounds normal. Only the secret agents know its secret meaning! You can make up plain codes with your fellow agents. For example, Agent A walks up to Agent B in a school playground. Are they safe and secure? Look at their conversation below – who else in the playground could guess what it means? Even enemies listening in wouldn't be suspicious. But what do our agents really mean?

Agent A:

'Are you playing soccer today?'

is code for:
'Are you OK for a dangerous job today?'

Agent B:

'Yes, I've brought my trainers'

is code for:
'Yes, I've got all my gear.'

Agent A:

'I'll go home and get mine'

is code for:
'See you at the park soon.'

You need to decide on other code phrases as well. For example, if Agent B added, 'Yes, but it looks like it's going to rain', this would be the signal to cancel your plans as there's danger somewhere!

Sneaky snares

Difficulty rating 🔒

Guard your secrets! Here's how to check if any baddies have been in your room...

HAS SOMEONE SNOOPED?

'Keep out!' If you want to see if someone's been snooping, snares are really useful. A snare is a kind of trap used, for example, by people catching animals. To spies, snares mean traps to catch out intruders. They don't actually capture the enemy but they warn you 'someone's been snooping!'

See where the lines join up?

Marked snare

Perhaps you leave things on a table in a muddle? No one will suspect there's a trap. You can make secret little marks that they won't spot. For example, if you have several things on a table or desk such as magazines or notebooks, you can draw a very thin line across between two of them. Set them so the line runs straight. If they're disturbed, you'll see that the line doesn't join up any more.

Hair snares

Leave a single hair in places where no one will notice it. If it has moved or is broken, you will know that your things have been moved or interfered with. Sometimes you will need to fix them in place with a tiny piece of tape or Blu-Tack.

Door or drawer

Put a hair at the bottom of a door or on one side of a drawer. Fix it with a small piece of tape or Blu-Tack. Or you can lick it and stick it!

Notebook

Put a hair at the bottom of one of the middle pages, bend it over and fold it into one of the earlier pages.

Case or bag

Zip up a case or backpack with a hair in the zip. If anyone opens it, you'll know as the hair will have gone!

Spy challenge

Can you think of any more hair snares?

Slip snares

Use small pieces of very thin pieces of paper about 1mm wide. If possible, use coloured paper to match the colour of the background as it's less likely to be noticed. If an intruder disturbs your things, you'll know as the slip will have slipped out!

Door

Put a small piece of paper in a door, either near the hinge or on the handle side, low down where people won't notice.

Letter

Put a small piece of paper at the bottom of a folded letter so it will drop out if disturbed. You can do this with a notebook too.

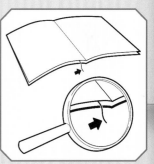

Drawer

Put a piece of paper at the front of a drawer. Bend it over so it stays in place when you leave it, but so that it will fall down when someone raids your possessions!

Lunchbox

Put a piece of paper between the two sides so that it's held in place when you close it. Now if anyone takes a look at your lunch, you'll know!

Soldier snares

Watch out for brothers, sisters or other suspicious characters in and around your home! Falling snares – like these special soldiers you can make – are things that fall or slip out of position, so an intruder can't hide his tracks.

PROJECT COMPONENTS

► Four different coloured markers

► Four toilet-roll tubes

► Four jam-jar lids in different colours

► Paper and pen

Set up this snare with sticks or a ruler

Pointing snare

Agent O seems to be leaving things in a bit of a mess. But he has arranged things quite carefully. His notebook is in line with the toy camper van and orange pen. If someone sneaks in and looks, he'll soon know!

1 To make your soldiers, draw a face or pattern on each of the cardboard tubes. Use only one colour per tube.

2 Decide which colour tube is to have which colour jam-jar lid or 'hat'. Put the lids on each tube, flat side down. Write down which colour soldier has which colour hat. Now set up your set of snares, close to the inside of your bedroom door. You need to stand them so that you can just squeeze out of the room!

3 They'll be knocked over by anyone coming in. The intruder will want to put them together again but won't know which 'hat' belongs to which 'soldier'. When you next enter your room (very carefully!) check your list and see if there's been a snooper.

Door trap

This is a different sort of snare. This time it scares the intruder – he'll realise you've caught him out. It will give someone a big surprise! To set this trap you first make a special small box. Then you fill it with things to drop on the enemy.

1 Cut a rectangle of paper. Fold the sheet in three. Fold it up at each end. As you fold, make a pair of triangular flaps. Fold these flaps over the box ends and fix with Sellotape.

2 Fill the box with some surprise stuff – for example, dry lentils, chickpeas or small pasta shapes. (Get adult permission first.)

3 Standing carefully on a chair, put the box on top of the door frame. Fix with two pieces of Sellotape, one short one that just goes onto the doorframe, and one long piece that stretches several centimetres onto the door.

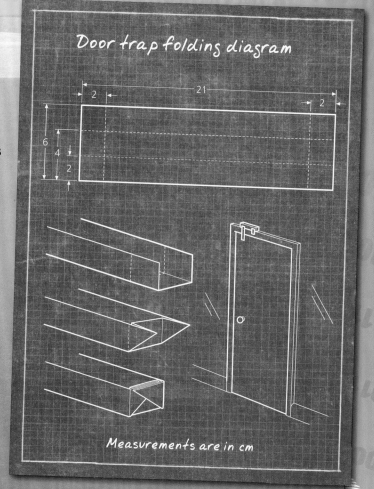

Door trap folding diagram

2   21   2

6 4 2

Measurements are in cm

Spy party games

If you get your spy ring together for a meeting, you need some games after the serious business is over. Here are a few to train you even better at the skills you need ...

Wink Assassin

Assassins are people who are paid to kill. They are paid by someone to assassinate (murder) a particular person. You wouldn't want a real assassin at your party! But this is a great game where you can play at being dead. It's best played with at least six players.

1 Cut out a few small rectangular pieces of paper, one for each player, and write a dot on just one. Fold up all the pieces so that the dot can't be seen, then put all the pieces in a bowl. Each player takes one. The person who gets the dot is the Assassin (but keeps it secret).

2 All players except one sit in a circle. This player is the Spymaster and can sit inside or outside the circle.

Try not to wink too obviously, Agent H!

3 Players look at each other while sitting in the circle. The Assassin 'kills' other players by winking at them! As soon as a player sees someone winking at him, he has to pretend to fall down dead. He can do this quietly or noisily.

4 The Spymaster has to spot the Assassin as soon as possible. As soon as he suspects someone, he says 'I accuse ———'. If he is right, the game starts again with a new Assassin and Spymaster; if he's wrong, the game continues – maybe until everyone has fallen down dead!

Catch Control

A Control tells other spies what to do. In this game, a Spy Catcher tries to catch Control. You need five or more players.

1 Everyone sits in a circle on the floor – they are the spies. The group picks a Spy Catcher, who then goes out of the room. The remaining spies choose someone to be Control.

2 The Spy Catcher is called back. He has to work out which player is Control. Control makes movements or signals that the others copy. The signals are silent – there's no talking except for pretend coughs and sneezes. Movements might be small or large. For example, small signals might be touching your nose; a bigger signal might be jumping up and down on one leg.

3 The Spy Catcher can ask everyone to stop by saying 'Calling Control, calling Control', which gives him a chance to watch very carefully as Control starts again. When Spy Catcher has found Control, he says, 'You're Control' and points to the player. If he's wrong, play continues until he finds the right person.

Spies' Liar Dice

Spies are very good at not telling the truth, which is useful in this game. You will need: two to four players, a pair of dice, a coffee mug and four counters for each player.

The aim of the game is to cheat but not get caught. To start, each player throws the dice; whoever scores highest starts.

1 Imagine you're Player 1. Using the mug, shake the dice and let them land still in the mug. You can see them but other players can't. Tell them the score. On this first go, you tell the truth. Let's say it's a total of 4.

2 Player 2 takes the dice and mug, and shakes them, making sure you cannot see. She needs a higher score, one or more higher than your first score. She can choose to lie or tell the truth, but has to claim it's a score higher than 4. Let's imagine she says she got 6.

3 Other players have to decide whether or not to believe her. If everyone believes her, play goes on. If you don't believe her, say "challenge". She has to show the dice. Was she lying? If the score is the same or more than she said, 6, you have to pay up, with a counter. She throws, starting again. But if the score was actually less than 6, she has to give you a counter, and the next player shakes the dice. He tries to get or pretends to get a higher score.

4 Once you reach 12, you can't go higher, so you start again at 2 or more and you keep jumping from 12 to 2 all through the game.

5 You're out when you've run out of counters.

Spy party

Contents

Fast fingers

Difficulty rating 🔒 🔒 🔒

Smart spies need to have rapid reactions. How quick are yours? Here's a way to see how fast you are with your fingers — how good are you at catching a moving target? This is a game for two players or more.

PROJECT COMPONENTS

- ▶ A4 sheet of paper
- ▶ Sellotape
- ▶ Marker pen
- ▶ Old pen

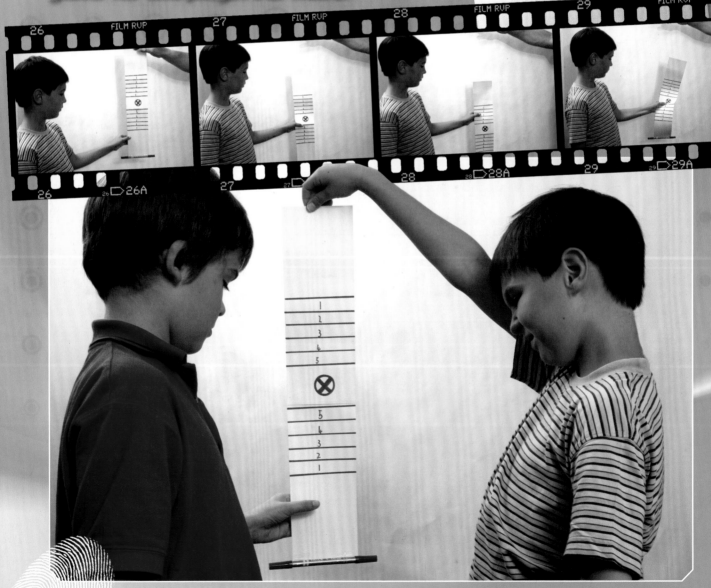

1 Fold the A4 sheet lengthways and cut in half. Tape the two short ends of the sheet together to make one long strip.

2 Copy the diagram. Draw a big cross in a circle on the seventh band down – that's your target. Write numbers on the other bands, as in the diagram. Colour in the bands if you like. Sellotape an old pen to the bottom.

3 To play, Player 1 holds the sheet high up in one hand. Player 2 puts his finger and thumb just to the side of the paper, at the bottom – but not touching the paper. Player 1 drops the paper through his fingers, and Player 2 has to catch it with his finger and thumb – as close to the target as possible. If he does, he scores 10 points. Now swap roles.

4 Once you've got the hang of the game, make it more difficult. For example, you can hold the paper higher; make Player 2 start with his fingers 15cm away from the paper; add a heavier weight to the paper so it falls faster.

Fast fingers diagram

1
2
3
4
5

⊗

5
4
3
2
1

2

4

Measurements are in cm

Spy invitations

Use spy language as in the example below: secret code for the party (can you guess why Firecake was chosen for this one?); spies like to use the 24-hour clock (what time does this party start and finish?); or give a coded rendezvous (RV2 means rendezvous point 2 – where would you like that to be?).

To: Agent M   From: Control

Urgent instructions:	Operation Firecake
Day:	Wednesday
Time:	1600 hours
Place	RV2 Secure
Getaway:	1800 hours

Invisible invitations
Write all invitations with invisible ink (see page 42) – and don't forget, tell your friends how to reveal the message or your secrets will stay with you!

Puzzling pieces
Write all the words on a card and then cut it into about ten pieces. Now your friends will have a jigsaw invitation to solve.

Muddling messages
You can use codes and micro messages (see pages 40–41). Remember to tell the recipients how to decode the message – if you don't they might miss the party!

Agent K's games

You may know Kim's Game, the memory game where you have to remember a collection of objects after they have been taken away. Agent K's memory games can be a bit trickier. When your spy ring gets really good at this, you can increase the number of objects to remember – how about trying to remember 20 different objects? This game requires you to look very carefully at things. You can play this in several ways.

PROJECT COMPONENTS

▶ Your choice of objects can include a pen, paper, piece of cutlery, book, magazine and secret message

▶ Edible paper and ink markers

▶ Sweets

Take one, Agent K

One player goes out of the room while another player takes one item away. The player who went outside comes back in and has to work out what has been removed. Then someone else gets a go until everything is off the table.

What's missing, Agent K?

In this version, one player is in charge of the objects. Everyone else has a minute to remember what's where, then they go out of the room. The player in charge removes one item. Everyone comes back in. The player who spots the change becomes the person to remove an item in the next round.

Just a minute, Agent K

Here, everyone takes turns. One player goes out of the room while the others remove one object and move one object. The player comes back into the room and tries to work out what's changed. Then someone else gets a go.

Take one, move one, Agent K

Everyone has pen and paper ready and everyone studies the objects for a minute. Then someone covers the items with a cloth. Everyone has to write down all the things they can remember. The winner is the one with the most complete list.

Eat your words, Agent K

Spies sometimes have to collect secret messages and then eat them to stop enemies finding them! Here's a game with edible paper so it's safe to eat your words! You need three or more players. You can buy edible paper and ink markers from kitchen and special cake-decorating shops and some larger supermarkets.

Agent H likes boiled eggs

1 Cut the edible wafer paper into small pieces, any shape, two per player. Using the edible ink marker, write down on each piece of edible paper some foods, for example, 'sausages and beans', 'bananas' and 'fish and chips'. Lay the paper on a table together with several different sorts of sweets. Keep a bag of spare sweets for prizes.

2 One person goes out of the room. One of the agents eats one of the pieces of paper or a sweet. The person comes back. If she can work out what's missing, she gets a prize of a sweet from the bag. Continue to take it in turns to guess what's missing until the table is empty.

Matchstick code trick

This trick relies on what magicians call 'distraction' – getting people to look in the wrong place so you can fool them. They will never guess how you do it!

PROJECT COMPONENTS

▶ **10 matches**
▶ **A table**

Chocolate game

Players sit in a circle on the floor. Put a bar of chocolate on a plate with a knife and fork next to it. Each player takes it in turns to roll the dice. When a player throws a 6, he immediately puts on all the clothes, tries to open the chocolate bar and eat pieces of chocolate using the knife and fork. Meanwhile, the other players keep rolling the dice. As soon as another player throws a 6, he takes the clothes off the other player, puts them on himself and continues trying to eat the chocolate with the knife and fork.

You will need: dice, chocolate, knife and fork, coat, scarf, hat and gloves

1 Explain to your audience that you have a special code they have to crack. Take six matches and put some of them on the table in a pattern – it doesn't matter what the pattern is. Tell them that this is the code for 3. When you have put the matches down, move one hand away from the matches but keep both of your hands on the table. Show three fingers on one hand, and tuck away the other fingers. Give your audience time to think.

2 Now move the matches – you can add or take away one if you like, changing the pattern a little. Tell them this is code for 4. Move one hand down out of the way again and with the other hand leave four fingers showing. Do this again, giving them a pattern which you say is 2. You show, of course, two fingers only on the table.

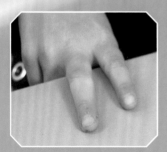

3 You can say that there is more than one way of showing the code for a number. So, put down a new pattern of matches and show four fingers. You can say that's matchstick code for 4.

4 Now, instead of telling them what number the matches represent, rest one or both of your hands on the table, showing however many fingers you like. Ask someone to guess what the number is.

5 If your audience can't guess the numbers, keep changing the pattern, adding or taking away matches. Put your hands down so the right number of fingers are showing and ask what the code is. Do not go above 8 too often as people are more likely to notice the trick. Don't put your hands too close to the matches. You can have a pattern of matches for 0 – move your hands away or make two fists. That will confuse them! As soon as someone has worked out the code they must whisper it to you or demonstrate it their way. Then you can let them have a go.

Question

Who do spies call when they make a mess?

Answer

The Cleaning Agents

Card games for spies

There can be a lot of waiting around when you're a spy, waiting and watching for people, waiting for the right moment to pounce! Card games are popular with spies young and old. Here are two old games for young spies to help you watch, wait and pounce.

PROJECT COMPONENTS

SNAP SLAPJACK

For 2–6 players:
▶ Standard pack of cards
▶ One joker

OLD SPY

For 3 or more players:
▷ Standard pack of cards
▷ One joker

Snap slap jack

1 Watch out for Jacks – they're the baddies! Deal the cards face down. Each player puts their cards into a pile face down. Player 1, left of the dealer, puts his top card in the middle of the table, turning it face up at the last moment. Others follow, building a pile of face-up cards, and all watch out…

2 As soon as someone plays a Jack – wham! Each player tries to be the first to slap a hand down on it. Whoever gets their hand there first takes all the cards from the middle pile and adds it to their stack. But beware: if you slap a card that's not a Jack, you have to pay a forfeit of two cards to each player.

3 If you run out of cards, you have one extra chance to slap and win another Jack. If you lose that, you're out. The player who ends up with all the cards is the winner.

The Joker is the Old Spy

Old Spy

1 The joker is the Old Spy. Shuffle the pack and deal out all the cards. Some players may have one or two more cards than the others, but it doesn't matter. Your aim is to collect pairs of cards and to avoid being left with the Old Spy.

2 Each player looks at their cards, making sure no one else sees, and puts down any pairs they already have, for example, two 6s or two Jacks, face up.

3 Player 1, left of the dealer, starts by holding up the rest of his cards without letting anyone see what they are. He offers them to Player 2 on the left, making sure he can't see them. Player 1 can try to encourage Player 2 to pick a particular card. Maybe it's Old Spy – maybe it isn't!

4 Player 2 picks one card and adds it to his hand. If it gives him another pair, he places it in front of him on the table. Then it's Player 2's turn to offer all his remaining cards to Player 3, making sure Player 3 can't see what they are. The game continues in the same way with the rest of the players.

5 Once you get rid of all your cards you're safe and you wait until the end of the game. The turn passes to the next player. Eventually all the cards will have been put on the table as pairs, except one – the lonely Old Spy (the joker). The person holding that card is the loser. The winner is the person with the most pairs. If you play again, the winner deals.

Dangerous drinks!

Difficulty rating 🔒 ▪ ▪ ▪ ▪

Drink can spell danger for spies! That's when the drink includes alcohol. If adults drink too much, they can get drunk, and they don't think clearly. But spies like to treat other people to drinks, especially alcohol, because contacts will relax – and maybe give away vital secrets!

PROJECT COMPONENTS

Lethal lime
▶ Drinking glass
▶ Half a lime
▶ Two teaspoons white sugar
▶ Drop of green food colouring
▶ Clear fizzy lemonade
▶ Slice of lemon

White lies
▶ Clear fizzy lemonade
▶ Slice of lemon

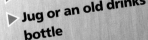

Wise whisky
▶ One tea bag
▶ Three teaspoons sugar
▶ Jug or an old drinks bottle

Lethal lime

Some spies and their contacts like cocktails. These are mixes of drink that are often very colourful and very, very alcoholic. This drink has such a bright green appearance that spies might suspect it was poisonous – however, although it may look lethal, it's simply safe and scrumptious! In a glass, squeeze the juice from the lime. Add the sugar, green food colouring and lemonade. Check the taste. Add extra sugar if you want. Decorate with a slice of lemon. Cheers!

"What's your poison?"

White lies

Gin, Martini and vodka are very alcoholic drinks with almost no colour. They are popular with spies. James Bond often ordered them ("shaken, not stirred") with fizzy drinks, which also have almost no colour, and drank them in a wide champagne glass. You can make you own young spy version easily. Put lemonade into a wine glass and decorate with a slice of lemon. Don't shake or stir! Plenty of people may think you're just like James Bond.

"Shaken, not stirred"

"Cheers!"

Wise whisky

Put the tea bag in a teapot or large mug. Boil a kettle, then carefully pour some boiling water onto the tea bag. Leave to brew for a few minutes. Take out the tea bag and add some sugar to taste. Leave to cool. Pour into a jug or bottle and then into a glass to make people think you're drinking whisky. Watch their faces – they may be shocked!

Secret-code cake

ADULT HELP NEEDED

If you're having a secret spy party, this is a great cake for all undercover agents. You can give them all a copy of the Morse code (see page 37) and whoever works out the code on the cake first gets a prize.

PROJECT COMPONENTS

CAKE MIX

▶ 175g/6oz softened margarine or butter (leave out of the fridge for an hour before cooking)
▶ 175g/6oz white sugar
▶ Three eggs
▶ Tablespoon of treacle
▶ Teaspoon vanilla essence

▶ Pinch of salt
▶ 80g/3oz cocoa, sifted
▶ 200g/7oz self-raising flour, sifted
▶ Six tablespoons apricot jam
▶ Two sandwich cake tins, 18cm diameter

ICING MIX

▶ 280g/8oz icing sugar, sifted
▶ Hot water
▶ Wooden spoon
▶ Bowl
▶ Sieve

If you have a food processor, you can mix all these ingredients in one go. Or you can beat them together using a wooden spoon or mixer in these stages:

▷ Mix the margarine and sugar well.
▷ Beat in the eggs.
▷ Mix in the treacle, vanilla essence, salt and cocoa.
▷ Stir in the sifted flour. Gently stir for a short time to mix thoroughly.

1 Preheat your oven to 190°C/375°F/gas mark 5. Line the tins with baking parchment (or, if they have a detachable base, grease them well). Divide the mixture evenly between the two tins.

2 Place mixture in the middle shelf of the oven for about 25 minutes. After 20 minutes, check if it's cooked. Stick a knife down in the middle. If the knife comes out clean, it's ready; if it comes out sticky, bake for another 5 minutes and test again. If still sticky, give it another few minutes.

3 Leave to cool, and then remove from the tin. Leave to cool further on a rack or plate.

4 When it's completely cool, spread apricot jam on one half and put the two halves together.

White icing

If you want to include some secret messages, put them in before you cover the cake with icing.

1 While you boil some water, sift the icing sugar into a bowl. Sift the cocoa into the bowl.

2 Add three tablespoons of hot water, and stir together.

3 The mixture will be very firm at first. Stir until you get a good, even consistency for spreading. Add a little more water, a teaspoonful at a time, if it's too thick. Spread the icing on the cake when it's cold and firm, with a flat knife.

Decoration

You can hide secret messages inside your spy cake before you put the jam or icing on. Use rice paper and edible ink markers, which you can get from cake-decorating shops and some larger supermarkets. Make sure you eat your cake on the same day, as otherwise your messages might get too soggy!

1 Cut out small pieces of rice paper and write on your secret messages (this could be in Morse code or perhaps a forfeit).

2 Cut slits in the sponge and gently push in your folded messages. Push them down into the cake so that the icing doesn't make them wet.

3 When you've iced the top of the cake, cut up liquorice string to make dashes and use sweets for your dots. It's a good idea to write out your code first, or lay out the sweets on some paper in the right order, so you don't make a mistake on the cake.

Make a pistol

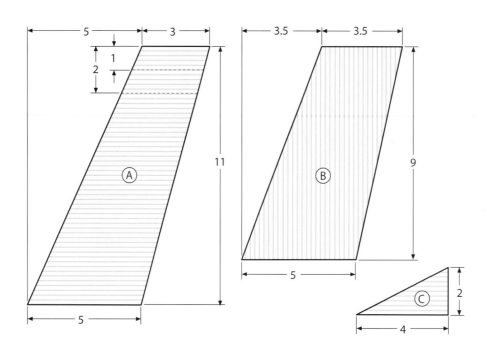

Super spy glider

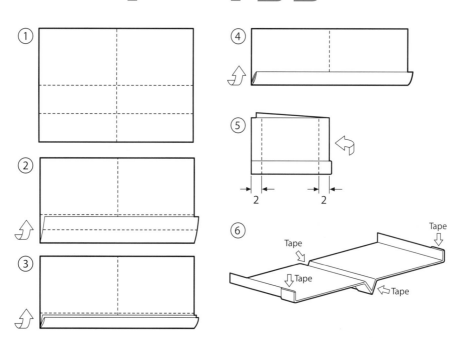

Sharpshooter gun

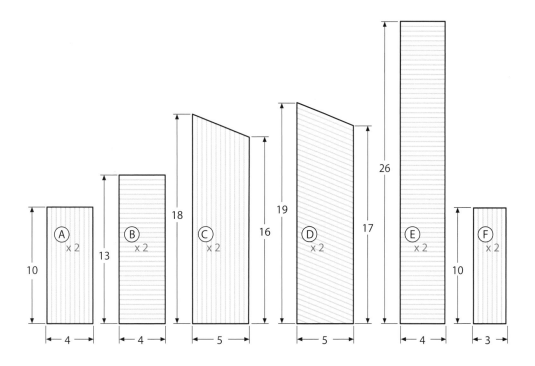

A ×2 — 10 × 4
B ×2 — 13 × 4
C ×2 — 18 / 16 × 5
D ×2 — 19 / 17 × 5
E ×2 — 26 × 4
F ×2 — 10 × 3

X ×3 — 12 sheets
Y — 24 sheets
W — 29.7 × 3 — 12 sheets
X ×3
Z — 12 sheets

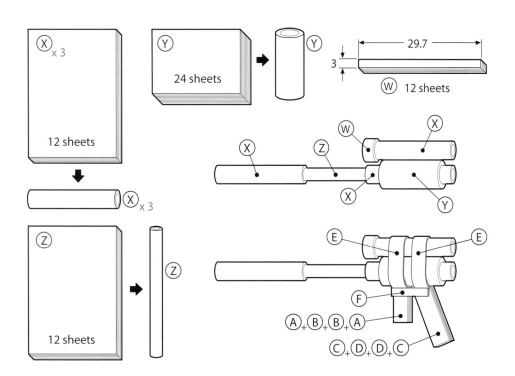

A + B + B + A

C + D + D + C

Morse code signaller

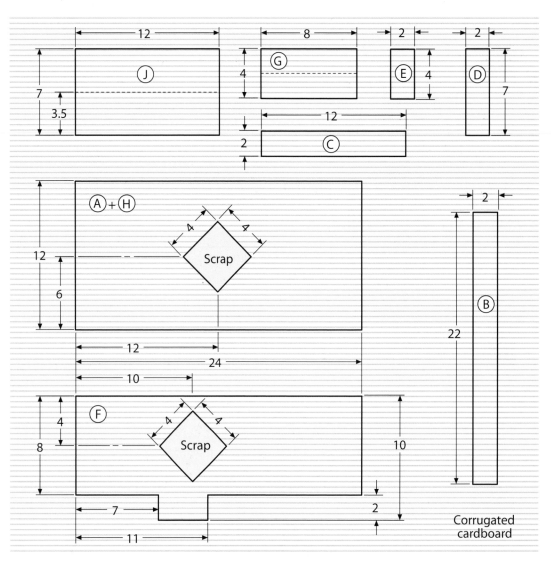

Corrugated cardboard

Assembly step 2

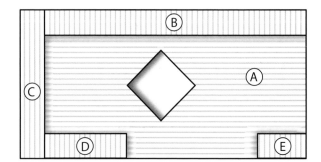